25 WALKS

IN

DOWN
DISTRICT

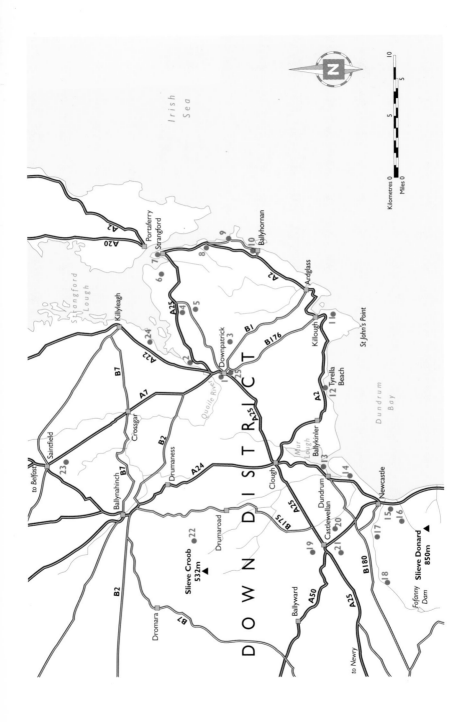

25 WALKS

IN
DOWN
DISTRICT

Leonard Lawson

Series Editor: Roger Smith

EDINBURGH: THE STATIONERY OFFICE

Applications for reproduction should be made to The Stationery Office

Acknowledgements

Thanks are due to the National Trust, Royal Society for the Protection of Birds, Department of Agriculture, Forestry Service, Down District Council, Environment and Heritage Service of the D.O.E. and the various landowners who have given their assistance by vetting text and supplying additional transparencies.

British Library Cataloguing in Publication Data

A catalogue record for this book is available from the British Library

ISBN 0 11 495773 8

CONTENTS

USEFUL INFORMATION

The length of each walk is given in kilometres and miles, but within the text the measurements are metric for simplicity. The walks are described in detail and are supported by accompanying maps (study them before you start the walk), so there is little likelihood of getting lost, but if you want a back-up you will find the Ordnance Survey 1:50,000 Discoverer maps on sale locally, as well as a few maps offering greater detail to selected areas.

Every care has been taken to make the descriptions and maps as accurate as possible, but the author and publishers can accept no responsibility for errors, however caused. Many walks in this book are along public rights of way, sections of the Ulster Way and permissive paths within specially managed visitor attractions. The countryside is always changing and there will inevitably be alterations to some aspects of these walks as time goes by. The publishers would be happy to receive comments and suggested alterations for future editions of the book.

General Information:
For information on accommodation, travel and visitor attractions contact the Tourist Information Centres at 74 Market Street, Downpatrick, Tel: 01396 612233 and Central Promenade Newcastle, Tel: 013967 22222.

Walk Information:
For further information on walking in Down District contact the Countryside Development Section of Down District Council, Tel: 01396 610800.

Appropriate Ordnance Survey Maps:-
Discoverer Series, scale 1:50,000: Sheets 21 'Strangford Lough', 19 and 29 'The Mournes'. Outdoor Pursuits Maps, scale 1:25,000; 'The Mournes' and 'Slieve Croob'.

Public Transport:
For details of public transport contact Ulsterbus, tel. Downpatrick 01396 612384 and Newcastle, 013967 22296

METRIC MEASUREMENTS

At the beginning of each walk, the distance is given in miles and kilometres. Within the text, all measurements are metric for simplicity (and indeed our Ordnance Survey maps are now all metric). However, it was felt that a conversion table might be useful to those readers who still tend to think in terms of miles.

The basic statistic to remember is that one kilometre is five-eighths of a mile. Half a mile is equivalent to 800 metres and a quarter-mile is 400 metres. Below that distance, yards and metres are little different in practical terms.

km	miles
1	0.625
1.6	1
2	1.25
3	1.875
3.2	2
4	2.5
4.8	3
5	3.125
6	3.75
6.4	4
7	4.375
8	5
9	5.625
10	6.25
16	10

INTRODUCTION

Down District is an area defined by the local authority boundary of Down District Council which is on the east side of Co. Down in Northern Ireland. The area has a beautiful coastline, rolling countryside, forest parks, rugged upland and Mountains. Each region has its own identity yet each is within a few kilometres of the other. It is in one of the most popular tourist areas in Ireland, 'The Coasts of Down', and contains a large and varied number of Visitor Attractions. This book is about walking in the countryside in an area renown for its friendliness, historic past, beauty and diversity.

Down with its rolling drumlin hills looks, from the air, like a basket of eggs. Three Areas of Outstanding Natural Beauty, several Nature Reserves and many Areas of Special Scientific Interest have all been designated within its boundary. Strangford Lough, a large inland waterway, forms the eastern boundary of the district, and has been designated the first Marine Nature Reserve in the United Kingdom.

Downpatrick is in the centre of the district and is the County Town. The main river flowing through the district, and past Downpatrick, is the Quoile River. To the south is the heartland of the patron saint of Ireland, Saint Patrick. It contains many religious and historic sites and a network of paths and roads known as St. Patrick's Way. Made up of a combination of scenic public footpaths and quiet country roads the network is very popular with walkers especially on St. Patrick's Day. Moving eastward away from Downpatrick and along the Quoile Estuary and the Lough shore is Castle Ward, one of the National Trust's most valued properties. The estate is famous for its large country house, castle and farm buildings in a magnificent park and woodland setting.

This area is part of the ancient Barony of Lecale and stretches out to the southeast of the district. Lecale is made up of rich and fertile farmland and a beautiful and varied coastline. Attractive seaside villages and towns on the shores of Strangford Lough and along the Irish Sea form that coastline. One of those villages is Strangford, a picturesque seaside port and the home of the Strangford Car Ferry. Connecting with the town of Portaferry on the Ards Peninsula, the ferry provides a wonderful opportunity for visitors to actually sail on Strangford Lough. This stretch of water, called the 'narrows', has one of the fastest flowing currents in the British Isles.

As you move southwestwards around the shoreline of the Irish Sea, you will notice a different coastal landscape, more rugged, with sea cliffs and sandy beaches. The coast of Down is famous for its abundant wildlife and scenic beauty. Ardglass and Killough are the main towns as you continue towards St. John's Point. A lighthouse on St. John's Point marks the start of Dundrum Bay which extends past Tyrella Beach, the town of Dundrum, Murlough Beach to the seaside resort of Newcastle. Behind these coastal fringes are areas of rich and fertile farmland, dotted with towns and villages that make up the lowland regions of the district.

The beautiful backdrop of the Mourne Mountains and to the north Slieve Croob dominates the landscape of Down District. You can see these two landmarks from almost any part of the district and form the western boundary. Below the mountains the gentle uplands with their forest parks provide excellent walking country. Towards the northern boundary the market towns of Ballynahinch and Saintfield are the major centres of population. Rowallane Garden in Saintfield is one of the National Trust's most famous gardens and one of the many visitor attractions in the district.

To complete the journey around Down District we return to the shores of Strangford Lough and Delamont Country Park. Delamont which is near the lough-side town of Killyleagh, just north of Downpatrick is the fastest growing visitor attraction in the district and is extemely popular for family outings. Its scenic paths move through gentle woodland, open countryside and along a picturesque foreshore.

I have picked these 25 walks to give a complete picture of Down District. The walks are suitable for most categories of walkers. They include quiet country lanes, forest tracks and coastal paths to formal parks and gardens. All are circular in nature and are a mixture of public and permissive paths and public highways. I have where possible tried to keep the walks off the roads so that you can enjoy the full countryside experience. Most of the walks, except the Mournes, are on lowland areas, usable all year around. While each season has its own character and its own beauty, if you want to get the best out of the countryside I always recommend spring and early summer.

LEONARD LAWSON

Other titles in this series

Long distance guides published by The Stationery Office

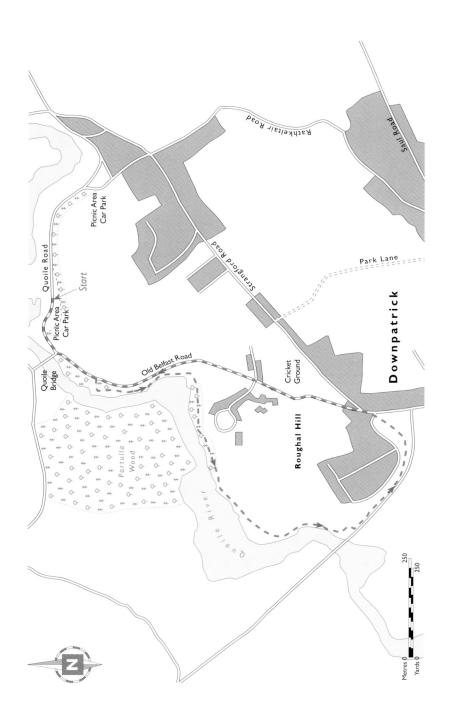

THE QUOILE RIVERSIDE —JANE'S SHORE

Quoile Riverside Walk is situated on the northern outskirts of Downpatrick, along the banks of the Quoile River. The walk consists of a riverside path managed by the Countryside Development Section of Down District Council, and the National Trust. The remainder is on footpaths adjoining the main road and public parkland. The Quoile River flows across the centre of Down District, past Downpatrick, then enters the sea at Strangford Lough.

Taking a walk along this route today, it is hard to believe that before 1957 the Quoile at this point was tidal. This is what made Downpatrick an important transportation and trading route. Ships, and thus cargoes, could get quite far inland compared with other ports around the coast. This was possible without too much navigational difficulty and in calm and peaceful waters.

After 1957 however coastal trade, already on its way out, was impossible, due to a tidal barrier being build across the estuary to control flooding. The Department of Agriculture built the barrier for two reasons. One was to stop flooding of agricultural land, thus making land on the banks of the river more productive. The second was to stop the flooding of Downpatrick which caused havoc during spring high tides.

This walk stretches along the Quoile from the Old Quoile Bridge to the New Quoile Bridge on the Belfast Road.

The river between these two points, although outside the Quoile Nature Reserve, is beautiful and full of wildlife. The Department of Agriculture manage the fishing rights and generally maintain the river and its banks. Outdoor centres use the river to teach people how to sail and canoe.

INFORMATION

Distance: 4.8km (3 miles).

Start and finish: At the car park/picnic site on the Quoile Road nearest the Old Quoile Bridge.

Terrain: Road, grass or dirt tracks and paths. Good walking shoes adequate. Some parts can still be wet after heavy rain.

Toilets: In the adjacent picnic area.

Refreshments: Cafes, restaurants and pubs in Downpatrick.

Public transport: Bus service from Downpatrick and Strangford. Car ferry from Portaferry.

Entrance to Downpatrick.

Begin the walk at the car park and picnic site on Quoile Road nearest to the Old Bridge. From here, cross the road to a path on the opposite verge that runs along the river towards the bridge. Take this path and when you reach the bridge, cross the main road and join the footpath on the other side, then walk towards Downpatrick. After a few hundred metres you will see a public footpath sign pointing away from the road towards the river. This path passes through a small wooded area to a larger open grass area beside the river and is a favourite picnic area known by the locals as 'Jane's Shore'. The origin of this name is unknown.

A newly constructed path runs from this point, along the banks of the Quoile, to the new bridge. This path was first envisaged by the late Lord Dunleath, a major landlord of the area. He saw it as an amenity for the people of Downpatrick to enjoy the peace and tranquility of the Quoile River. Unfortunately he died before the path was constructed. His land agent and other landowners along the river, with the assistance of the Department of Agriculture and Down District Council, made his vision come true. The first section parallel to the Old Belfast Road is managed by the National Trust and the remainder by the Countryside Development Section of Down District Council.

Wildlife on the Quoile.

Start walking along this first section of path, which is bordered with trees and thick undergrowth on one side and reed beds on the other. It meanders along the natural shape of the river. Small sections of the path are still subject to flooding once or twice a year. As a result timber boardwalks were constructed where it would have been difficult to find a firm, dry surface to walk on. A few metres after you walk over the first boardwalk, the path widens into a large grassy area. This is part of a recreation area for a nearby housing development.

Continue across this area and through a timber kissing gate into an adjoining field. From here the path is fenced off on both sides and young trees have been planted to form a hedge along the fence line. Gaps have been made in the fencing to allow livestock to cross to the river. These gaps can be negotiated by a system of kissing gates which allow you to pass yet keep the livestock off the path. You will also notice several small stiles crossing the path. These are for anglers whose rights of passage were established long before the new route was made. The levels of the path and the design of the kissing gates make the route usable by the disabled and wheelchair users.

As you follow the path along the river, look at the wildlife in the reed beds and on the open water. Continue until you arrive at the new bridge on the Belfast Road. A path will take you up the side of the bridge onto the grass verge of the main road . This is a wide verge planted with roses to decorate the entrance to the town. Walk along the dust path provided towards Downpatrick.

Where the dust path ends, go through an opening in a timber fence. Turn right and through a small public park, called Roughal Park. Stay on the paved path that leads to the

View across the Quoile with Slieve Croob in the background.

centre of the park, which is simply landscaped with trees, rose and shrub beds. Near the centre is a sculpture commissioned by the Council to represent Downpatrick. It is a modern Celtic-type cross set in the middle of a circular, stone-walled, raised area. After passing this feature, keep to the left and take the path that leads towards the eastern exit from the park. Once on the footpath, keep left again past the War Memorial along the Old Belfast Road.

The road will take you past the town's cricket club and the Down Academy. Walk over a small hill past the entrance of a small housing development, past some private dwellings, and then downhill back towards the river. At the bottom of the hill, walk along the footpath back towards the old bridge. Cross the road onto the path opposite the car park where the walk began.

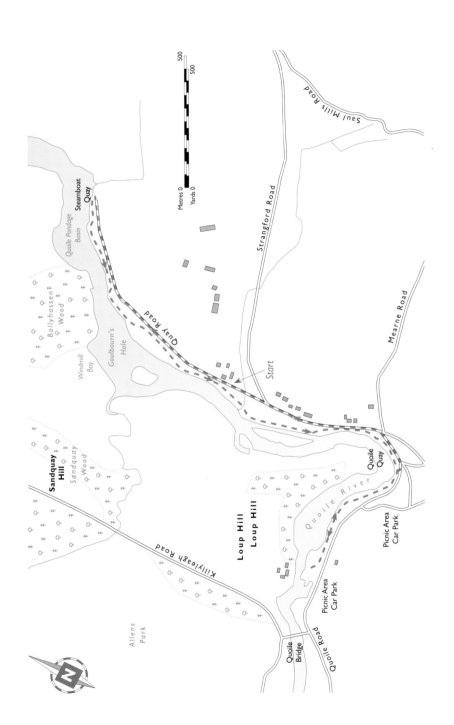

Steamboat Quay

Quoile Pondage Basin

Ballyhassen Wood

Windmill Bay

Goulbourn's Hole

Quay Road

Start

Strangford Road

Saul Mills Road

Mearne Road

Sandquay Hill

Sandquay Wood

Quoile Quay

Loup Hill
Loup Hill

Quoile River

Picnic Area Car Park

Picnic Area Car Park

Killyleagh Road

Allens Park

Quoile Bridge

Quoile Road

Metres 0   500
Yards 0   500

QUOILE PONDAGE NATURE RESERVE

Quoile Pondage Nature Reserve is situated on the banks of the Quoile River, on the outskirts of Downpatrick, just off the main Strangford Road. The Rivers Agency, part of the Department of Agriculture, own most of the reserve and manage it in conjunction with the Environment and Heritage Service, an agency of the Department of the Environment. The 'Quoile Pondage' is a basin, on the estuary of the River Quoile, where floodwaters can gather before discharging into Strangford Lough at each low tide.

The construction of a tidal barrier in 1957 dramatically changed the environment from salt water to freshwater. Marsh plants naturally established themselves on the former seashore, growing along the river banks. Reed-beds and rushy grassland with alder or willow scrub now dominate the muddy bays. Woodland of oak and ash is developing on the higher stony shores. Near the barrier the river broadens out into a brackish lake.

An excellent site for bird watching, the Quoile attracts migrating wading birds in spring and autumn. In summer, swans and many breeding wildfowl appear, including the scarce gadwall. You can view large numbers of widgeon and ducks in winter. The area is rich in insects, providing food for fish such as rudd and eels. In turn grey herons, cormorants and grebes feed

INFORMATION

Distance: 4.8km (3 miles).

Start and finish: At the car park beside the Quoile Information Centre, which is signposted off the main Downpatrick/Strangford road (A25), 2.5km north-east of Downpatrick.

Terrain: Road, footpath, grass and metalled paths. Good walking shoes generally adequate. Some stretches can be wet after heavy rain.

Toilets: At the Information Centre, and at one of the recreation/picnic areas along the route.

Refreshments: Shops, restaurants and pubs in Downpatrick.

Opening hours: The reserve is open all year, free. The Information Centre opens 1100-1700 daily Apr-Sep and 1100-1700 Sat/Sun only Oct-Mar. Groups by arrangement. For further information tel 01396 615520.

Public transport: Bus service from Downpatrick and Strangford.

Quoile Countryside Centre.

on them. There is a splendid bird-watching hide
down-river at Castle Island Road.

The Quoile estuary is also rich in history. It was a port
supplying the town of Downpatrick, which was the
administrative and government centre of the county.
St Patrick used its waters to gain access to the area and
set up his church. John de Courcy, the Norman
Knight who conquered the area, used it to supply the
town. Subsequent military governors of the area did
the same. Two old quays and timbers of an old sailing
ship remain as evidence of its maritime past.

Within the Reserve is a Countryside Centre. This is a
base for the local Environment and Heritage Service
Warden and staff who look after this and other
reserves in the district. The Centre is based in a
renovated cottage that stands beside Quoile Castle,
which was built around 1600.

To start the walk, leave the car park and turn right along
Quay Road. Follow the road, bordered on each side with
hedges and trees, past two picnic areas. After the second
picnic site, take a small track to the left towards the river.
This leads to the 'Steamboat Quay' where the old sailing
vessels would have unloaded their cargo. In the late
1830s, a paddle steamer service to Liverpool operated
from here. The Quay marks the northerly boundary of
public access to this section of the Reserve.

From the Quay, go down to the lower path that runs
along the edge of the river. Follow the path through
secluded areas of trees and past the picnic areas and reed
beds. The walk is very peaceful here, and the vegetation
cover makes it an ideal place to observe the abundance
of wildlife. Stay on the lower path and make your way
over a small wooden bridge and past the timbers of an
old sailing ship, the Hilda. The path ends a short
distance later when you arrive at the 'Coal Quay'.
Climb the steps on to the quay and take the dust path at
the top across a large grass area next to a small layby.

Continue along the path, which is parallel to the road
and flanked with a wooden fence. A feature of the

path is the boardwalk and small outcrops of banking, along the river bank, built to facilitate anglers. These facilities are positioned at intervals along the entire route. On the other side of the river, reed beds dominate the landscape, backed by natural woodland. This makes the walk very scenic, and the reflection of the trees across the water is one of its unique features. Opposite the path, on the other side of the road, are two large picturesque recreation areas with car parks and picnic sites, again backed with beautiful trees. Both are managed by Down District Council.

As the path makes its way around the bend in the river, it leaves the side of the road and drops to just above the level of the river. After a few hundred metres it rejoins the road verge and returns to road level. A short distance later, on the right, there is a purpose-built facility for disabled anglers. Above it are the 'Old Floodgates' used to control the flooding that used to be a feature of the area. This marks the end of the reserve.

Return along the path back to the 'Coal Quay'. Do not go down the steps on to the riverside walk. Instead, keep to the footpath until it joins the Strangford Road. Continue on this footpath back towards the Centre. From this elevated route you get a panoramic view of the river and the Reserve.

Steamboat Quay.

Follow the Strangford Road until it veers off to the right. At this point leave the road and follow the signposted route, down Quay Road, back to the Information Centre and the car park where the walk began.

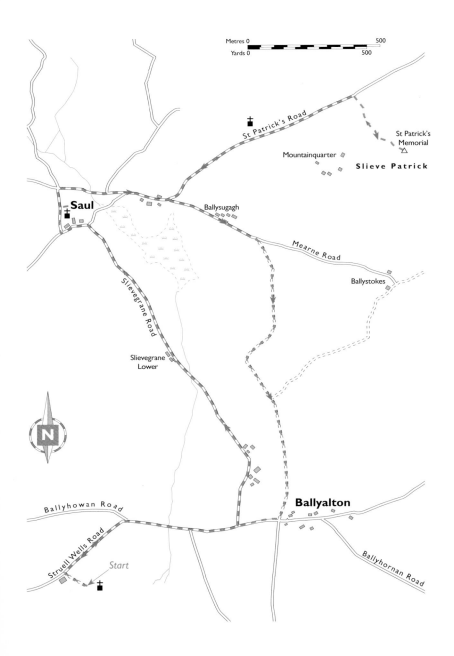

Metres 0   500
Yards 0   500

St Patrick's Road

St Patrick's
Memorial

Mountainquarter

Slieve Patrick

Saul

Ballysugagh

Mearne Road

Ballystokes

Slievegrane Road

Slievegrane
Lower

N

Ballyalton

Ballyhowan Road

Struell Wells Road

Start

Ballyhornan Road

ST PATRICK'S WAY - STRUELL AND SLIEVE PATRICK

Saint Patrick's Ecclesiastical Trail is a journey around the churches and shrines in and around the parish of Saul, just outside Downpatrick. Saul was the townland in which St Patrick founded his original church, and from where he spread Christianity in Ireland. You don't have to be religious to enjoy this walk - it just so happens that it travels through some of the nicest countryside in Ireland.

The walk is a mixture of visiting ecclesiastical sites, old and quite recent, exploring history, getting healthy exercise and viewing the countryside. Most of the route is on quiet roads, country lanes and grassy hillsides.

Start the walk at the car park at Struell Wells, which is an early Christian site visited by St Patrick. It consists of the remains of an old church, a drinking well, an eye well, and bath houses for men and women. The waters are said to have healing properties. Leave the wells by walking down the entrance road and on to the Struell Wells Road. Turn right and walk towards the Ballyhornan Road. At the junction with this road, turn right, away from Downpatrick. Continue along this slightly busier road until you reach the first road junction on the left. This is the Slievegrane Road. Take this road and follow it in a northerly direction towards Saul. It is a quiet road, elevated above the surrounding hills and provides beautiful views across the countryside to the north and east.

INFORMATION

Distance: 12km (7.5 miles).

Start and finish: At the car park at Struell Wells which is signposted off the Ardglass Road (B1) and the Ballyhornan Road 4km outside of Downpatrick.

Terrain: Mainly road, some grass/dust tracks and paths. Good walking shoes or boots recommended can be muddy and uneven.

Toilets: None the nearest public toilets are in Downpatrick.

Refreshments: Shops, pubs and restaurants in Downpatrick. Pubs, shop and restaurants on the route.

Opening hours: No restriction on the route or the Wells.

Public transport: Bus service from Downpatrick and Strangford. Car ferry from Portaferry.

Struell Wells.

Saul Parish Church.

At the end of the road turn left and on to the Saul Road. From the top of this hill you get a really good view of Strangford Lough and the Ards Peninsula on the far shore. A short distance later, turn right down a very steep hill. Here you will notice the distinctive round tower of the St Patrick's Memorial Church, a Church of Ireland parish church.

Leave the road at this point and walk around the church and graveyard. The church was build on the spot where Patrick was reputed to have been given a barn by the local chieftain Dichu and where he in turn established his first church. There is a special service here every St Patrick's Day that marks the start of a long day of celebration.

The old part of the graveyard is very ancient indeed and a lot of the graves are marked merely by stones in the ground. A special feature of the graveyard is an old Mortuary. After leaving this spot turn right and walk downhill. At the bottom turn right on to the Mearne Road. This will take you past the Countryside Inn, a popular pub and restaurant, open unfortunately only on certain days. A quick phone call before setting off could avoid disappointment. Carry on past some modern bungalows, a small housing estate on your right and back out into the open countryside.

A couple of kilometres further on, you reach St Patrick's Roman Catholic Church on the left. The church contains within its walls a stone from the original church built by Patrick. It also has a fine stained glass window depicting the arrival of Patrick by boat. From here you will see on top of a hill opposite the most famous landmark of the area, a statue of St Patrick. This statue and its associated shrines are floodlit at night.

Leave the chapel and continue down this road for a few hundred metres and you will find the entrance to these shrines and a grass path that will take you to the top of the hill and the statue. The base of the monument is decorated with bronze panels depicting scenes from the saint's life. This is a steep hill but I am sure the penance of climbing it will do you no harm. Whether you are religious or not the climb is absolutely worth it. The hill is called Slieve Patrick, after the saint. However it was not always so and older maps of the area show the hill as Slievewellian.

Quite apart from the climb, the views from the top of the hill are heart-stopping. The panorama is fantastic and takes in the coast from the Mournes to St John's Point, Ballyhornan and the entrance to Strangford Lough, the Ards peninsula and Strangford Lough, the Belfast hills and Slieve Croob. Finally, looking in the same direction as the saint you will see the town of Downpatrick, with its Church of Ireland Cathedral, where St Patrick is allegedly buried.

After a short rest, walk back down the hill and on to the road. Turn left and walk back past the chapel. Keep walking until you come to the Mearne Road on your left at a very sharp bend in the road. Turn left and walk up this road. The road is rather like a farm lane and serves only a few dwellings. Follow it until you see a public footpath sign on the right that directs you over a stile and on to a farm lane.

Continue along the lane through the peaceful countryside with its beautiful stone dykes and surrounding green fields. The lane is only used by local farmers and ramblers and forms part of the St Patrick's Way network of paths. After a considerable distance the lane is joined by another lane on the left. Ignore it and continue walking straight ahead.

The path eventually brings you to Ballyalton, a small settlement of houses on the Ballyhornan Road. Climb the wooden stile at the end of the lane. Turn right and walk down the Ballyhornan Road, past the Slievegrane Road, until you again reach the sign for Struell Wells. Retrace your steps from this point back to the Wells and the car park where the walk began.

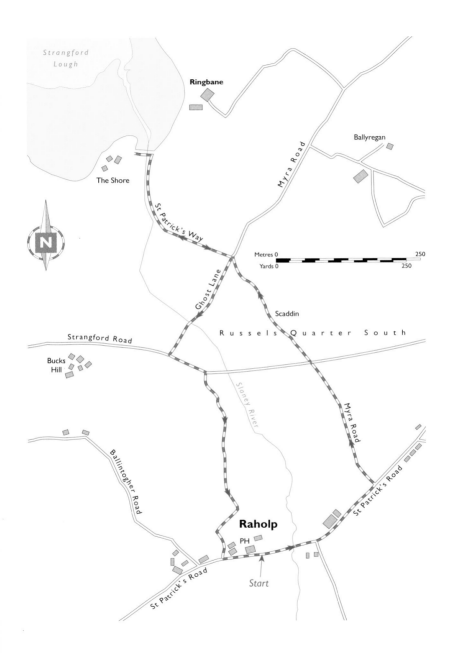

ST PATRICK'S WAY - RINGBANE

Saint Patrick's Way is a network of paths and roads through the countryside a few kilometres outside the County Town, Downpatrick. The walk takes you to the saint's first landing place in Ireland, where he preached and established his first church and converted the first Irish Chieftains to his form of Christianity. The nearby town of Downpatrick is the alleged burial place of the saint.

The first walk includes the townland of Raholp and the shores of Strangford Lough. It is through rich agricultural land which, although hilly due to the drumlin landscape, is ideal for walkers. Each year on St Patrick's Day, Down District Council along with the local Lecale Rambling Club organise a walk through this area. It is very popular and attracts hundreds of visitors. Organisers distribute a local brew during the walk and they still cannot say, hands on hearts, if it is the walk or the brew that attracts the participants.

Begin the walk at the car park of the Slaney Inn, a public house and restaurant in the small village of Raholp. As you leave the car park, turn left towards the town of Strangford. Then take the first road on your left, which is Myra Road. Continue along this road until you reach the main Strangford Road. Cross straight over at the crossroads, with care, and walk straight ahead, still on Myra Road. The road is quite narrow with little traffic, but you should always be prepared to meet something.

As you walk downhill towards Strangford Lough, the views are quite stunning, especially across the lough and farmland surrounding it. At the bottom of the hill, turn left off Myra Road on to a small road that leads down to the lough shore. This is the townland of Ringbane. Continue down this road and at the bottom of the hill go through a gate on your right. A

INFORMATION

Distance: 4.3km (2.75 miles).

Start and finish: Car park, Slaney Inn, Raholp, about 6km east of Downpatrick, just south of the Strangford-Downpatrick road (A25).

Terrain: Road, tracks, paths and foreshore. Strong shoes or boots recommended, as the ground can be muddy and uneven in places.

Refreshments: Shop and pub in Raholp. Wider choice in Strangford and Downpatrick.

Public transport: Bus service from Downpatrick and Strangford. Car ferry from Portaferry.

Walking from the shore towards Slieve Patrick.

grass and soil track leads you along the banks of the Slaney River, down to a barrier. The barrier sits on the foreshore and prevents the salt waters of the lough flooding onto the agricultural land on each side or the river.

St. Patrick landed on this foreshore in 432 AD. It was here he first met the local chieftain and befriended him. From this point he made his way upstream to a barn where he established his first church.

Rest a while at this location and ponder the moment when this happened. Look across the estuary of the Quoile River, the islands and the far shore. Breathe in the sea air and wonder at the scenery. Observe and listen to the wildlife on the lough, the foreshore and in the hedgerows. Watch the animals in the fields. This is what walking in the countryside is about. All around you is historical legend, natural wildlife, peace and tranquility.

When you are ready, retrace your footsteps back to the road, turn left and walk back uphill to the junction with the Myra Road. At this point you will see a public footpath signpost directing you towards a wooden stile on your right. Go over the stile and onto a grass lane. Follow the lane between two hedgerows

The estuary of the Slaney River where St Patrick landed in Ireland.

back towards the Strangford Road. Some locals call this lane 'Ghost Lane'.

The road to Ringbane.

The lane can be quite muddy in places, and the River Slaney crosses it about two-thirds of the way up. However, the river is very narrow at this point and is crossed by a small footbridge. After this, the lane climbs steeply uphill to another wooden stile and then joins the Strangford Road.

Cross the road, taking due care as this is a busy and fast stretch of road. Turn left and walk downhill to face the oncoming vehicles. About 40 m down the road, a public footpath sign directs you over a stone stile and into a field. No definitive path exists at this point. Walk straight ahead for about 30 m before veering to the right and up the steep bank to the ditch above. Follow this ditch along the top of the bank until you come to another stile. Go over the stile and into the next field.

A waymark sign at the stile directs you across another field. Walk out into the field as shown, over the crest of a hill and then on to the corner of the ditch opposite. Continue walking along the ditch to the corner of the field. Here you will find a stone stile that takes you into a lane. Follow this lane in a southerly direction back towards the village of Raholp. As you near the houses, the lane turns sharp right and uphill. It then veers left and passes between some outhouses and along the side of a house on to St Patrick's Road.

This brings you right into the heart of the village. Turn left at St Patrick's Road and walk downhill about 60 m to the Slaney Inn and the car park where the walk began - and perhaps some well-earned refreshment.

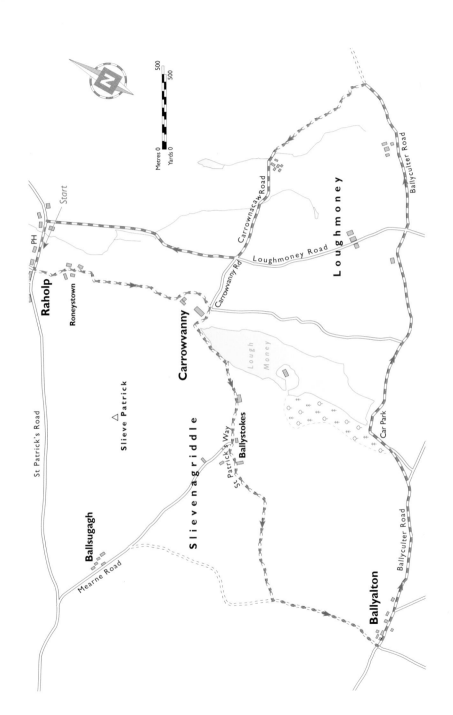

ST PATRICK'S WAY - LOUGH MONEY

This walk follows another section of the Saint Patrick's Way network. This time the walk is to the south of St Patrick's Road and around a freshwater lake called Lough Money. The walk passes through agricultural land of a different type from the previous area of the network. Except for Lough Money, the land is higher and the landscape is more rugged and inhospitable. It is, however, just as pleasant to walk through and, because of its elevation, just as pleasing from the scenic point of view.

Apart from the annual walking festival on St Patrick's Day, Down District Council organises special guided walks and has produced a special leaflet on walking in the area. St Patrick's Way is ideal for walking as it is steeped in history, especially of the religious kind. To supplement this it has a good supply of pubs, restaurants and shops spread out around the area.

The walk begins once again, in the car park of the Slaney Inn, at the centre of the village of Raholp. Leave the car park and turn right up the hill. Take the first lane on your left, only a few metres from the pub. Walk up this lane past the small farm dwellings and outbuildings of Roneystown. Once you pass these buildings the lane turns sharp right, uphill, then left, allowing you to continue in a southerly direction. On your right is Slieve Patrick, on top of which is a statue of the saint. This is a landmark for the whole area as it stands on one of the highest hills in the district.

Proceed along the lane until you arrive at a large farm. Walk through the farm and on to the Carrowvanny Road. Turn right at this point and walk downhill past a very well kept farmhouse with a beautiful garden. In spring and summer, lovely

INFORMATION

Distance: 9.6km (6 miles).

Start and finish: Car park, Slaney Inn, Raholp. See Walk 3 for directions.

Terrain: Road, tracks, paths and foreshore. Strong shoes or boots recommended as some parts can be muddy and uneven.

Refreshments: Shop and pub in Raholp. Wider choice in Downpatrick and Strangford.

Public transport: Bus service from Downpatrick and Strangford. Car ferry from Portaferry.

Slievenagriddle.

blooms of wallflowers appear in the stone walls and along the grass verges. The forested side of Slievenagriddle rises steeply in the background, its hillside contrasting beautifully with the surrounding landscape.

After you pass the farm, the road veers to the left and a short distance later you reach the shores of Lough Money. This is a beautiful little lough managed by the Department of the Environment, Water Service. It is popular with anglers, who fish under licence from the Department of Agriculture. The Department also manage fish stocks and monitor usage by fishermen. It is also a popular habitat for wildlife, which get a chance to feed and breed in peaceful surroundings.

Walk along the lane beside the lake until you reach a gate restricting access to the rest of the lough shore. Beside the gate, a public footpath sign directs you uphill, away from the lough. Follow the signs and walk up the hill, looking back at the lough and the surrounding countryside. Eventually you will arrive at some farm buildings, at the townland of Ballystokes.

Ignore a lane that branches off to the right and continue to keep left around the buildings. Climb over the stile at the side of the house and follow the lane into the open countryside. The lane from here can be muddy in places, although most of the surface is grass. On your left you will see the other side of Slievenagriddle which is less prosperous, yet more natural than the forested side you saw from the lough shore. The lane is lined with picturesque stone walls which are a feature of the area.

After some distance the lane meets another, at right angles. Turn left here. This lane will eventually lead

Looking from Ballyalton to Slievenagriddle.

you through a gateway, over a wooden stile and on to the Ballyhornan Road. Turn left here and walk past the houses, pub and shop that form the small settlement known as Ballyalton or the 'Road Houses'. Continue walking until you reach the next road junction. Take the Ballyculter Road, a minor road branching to the left, and follow it down and around several bends to the bottom of the hill. As you near the bottom you will again see the forest on your left and Lough Money straight ahead.

There is a small car park just at the corner of the road on the lough shore. This is the southern end of the lough, and you get a wonderful view over the water to the opposite end. On a still day the reflection of the forest and the hillside in the water is superb. In the centre of the lake you will notice a small building. This is a pump house that sits on a small headland. It is used by the Water Service to control water extraction and levels within the lough.

Leave the car park and walk uphill past the next road junction and straight ahead at the crossroads. Again I will stress that it is as important to look behind you as to look ahead, if you want to get the best from the views. The route will begin to climb again; keep going until, about 2.5km from the lough, you find a signpost indicating another public footpath, on your left. This is a narrow, hedge-lined path that starts to bring you

Lough Money.

back towards Lough Money. Follow this path as it winds its way around the field boundaries until you reach the Carrownacaw Road.

Once on this road, keep left until it joins the Lough Money Road. At this junction, turn right. Don't forget to look over the hedge to see a perfectly preserved Dolmen, or chambered tomb, reminding us once again that we were not the first to find this beautiful spot. Continue walking to the end of the Lough Money Road, to the junction with St Patrick's Road. Then turn left and up the hill a few hundred metres to the Slaney Inn car park, where the walk began.

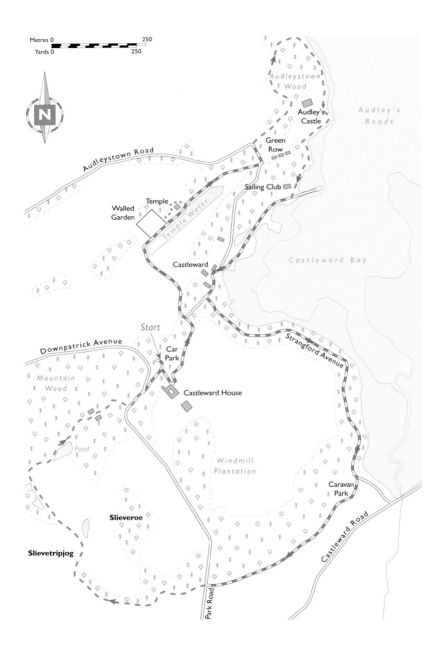

Metres 0 — 250
Yards 0 — 250

N

Audleystown Wood

Audley's Castle

Audley's Roads

Green Row

Audleystown Road

Sailing Club

Temple Water

Temple

Walled Garden

Castleward Bay

Castleward

Start

Strangford Avenue

Downpatrick Avenue

Car Park

Mountain Wood

Castleward House

Pond

Windmill Plantation

Caravan Park

Slieveroe

Castleward Road

Slievetripjog

Park Road

CASTLE WARD

Castle Ward is a National Trust property situated on the shores of Strangford Lough and the eastern side of Down District. It has been in the Ward family for 12 generations and is one of the Trust's most popular visitor attractions in Northern Ireland.

The estate consists of a large mansion (famous for its architecture - one side Classical style, the other in Gothic), landscaped gardens, extensive stretches of foreshore, woods and farmland.

Enter the estate by the main Ballyculter Gate Lodge, and follow the drive as shown to the main car park. Just opposite the entrance is a sign that states 'Stable Yard'; take this route. In the stable yard is an information office. Reading some literature about the estate or visiting the main house before walking will make your walk even more enjoyable.

Leaving the stable yard, follow the sign for the Farmyard. This is a delightful path which leads you downhill under a bridge and away from the main buildings. A finger-post sign halfway down the track points to the Temple Water. Take this route under another bridge to a second finger-post and the start of the Lime Avenue.

At the end of the tree-lined avenue, you will find the Temple Water. Looking down the lake you get your first view of Audley's Castle, a 15th century Anglo-Norman Tower House.

Follow the path along the side of the lake past the former walled garden. At this point it is worth taking a slight diversion to your left, then right and uphill, to enjoy the views from the 'Temple' situated above the lake. Return to the track and continue until you reach a gate that leads on to a tarmac road.

Turn left up the hill, at the top turn

INFORMATION

Distance: 8km (5 miles).

Start and finish: Main car park, Castle Ward, signposted off the A25 road, 1.5km from Strangford.

Terrain: Roads, tracks and paths. Strong shoes or boots recommended as parts of the walk can be muddy.

Toilets: Stable Yard and Old Farmyard.

Refreshments: Restaurant in Stable Yard. Wider choice in Strangford and Portaferry.

Public transport: Bus service from Downpatrick and Strangford. Car ferry from Portaferry.

Opening hours: Grounds open all year, daily. House, Victorian Pastimes Corner and Laundry, Cornmill, Wildlife Centre, shop and restaurant open Mar-Oct. Hours vary, enquire locally or tel 01396 881204. Admission charge. N.T. Members free.

Castle Ward Farmyard.

Castle Ward, Temple Water.

right, towards Audley's Castle, through another gateway or climb over the stile provided. Follow the dirt track until it ends at a gate below the castle. The castle is worth a visit and the view from the top, of Castle Ward Bay, the narrows of Strangford Lough, the Ards peninsula and town of Portaferry are breathtaking.

At the gate, turn left and take a grass path marked by two large stones. The path takes you away from the castle and into Audley's Wood. Follow the path through the woods until it doubles back to join the shores of the lough. Continue on the path along the shoreline until you reach a gate and stile. Climb over the stile and into a field. Again keeping parallel to the shoreline, walk until you reach a kissing gate. Go through the gate on to a track which leads past a small slipway back towards the Green Row Cottages.

Before reaching the entrance to the cottages turn left, keeping to the foreshore (can you spot the secret passage?). This will lead to a path which passes Strangford Sailing Club, the Lead Quay, boathouses, a beautiful estate cottage and eventually a picnic site. At the other end of the picnic site, an archway marks the entrance to the farmyard.

As you pass through the archway, a clock tower opposite dominates the old farmyard and marks the entrance to a courtyard car park. On each side of the entrance road are small cottages, a fully restored Corn Mill and a Sawmill. Outside the courtyard are various other buildings used in the past for the storage of farm carts and equipment.

Leave the farmyard complex by following the sign for the House. As you walk uphill, on your left is a converted barn now used by the Trust as the Strangford Lough Wildlife Centre.

Continue walking uphill until you reach a path on the left marked Lough Side Walk. Take this route, which follows the estate boundary wall and the shoreline of Castle Ward Bay towards the village of Strangford.

Stay with the path until it reaches a wooden gate at the side of a caravan and camping site. At the entrance to the site is a car park. A small waymark post with the Trust's acorn leaf and a black arrow directs you to the rear of the car park. Here you will find an opening to a grass path which leads uphill through coniferous woodland and along the boundary wall to the main entrance road.

Look for a similar waymark post which directs you across the road to another grass path. This path is less well defined and again passes through coniferous woodland at the side of the Ballyculter Gate Lodge. At a fork in the path, keep left as shown by the black arrow on the waymark post. Continue until you leave the wood, then pass through an opening at the side of a new plantation. Here the path again follows the boundary wall. When you are clear of the trees, have a look over the wall for a striking panoramic view of the surrounding countryside.

The path leads to another wooded area on your left and passes two small ponds. It then enters a broadleaved wood where you will find on your right a large natural pond. As the path leaves the side of the pond, keep to the path that veers to the right. A short distance later you will find

Castle Ward.

another waymark post with a black arrow which directs you over a small hill towards some buildings known as the Basecamp (formerly Keepers Cottage).

Pass between the buildings and take the path downhill towards the main house. Follow the path, turning to the left where it joins the main entrance road. From here it is only a short distance to the main car park where the walk started.

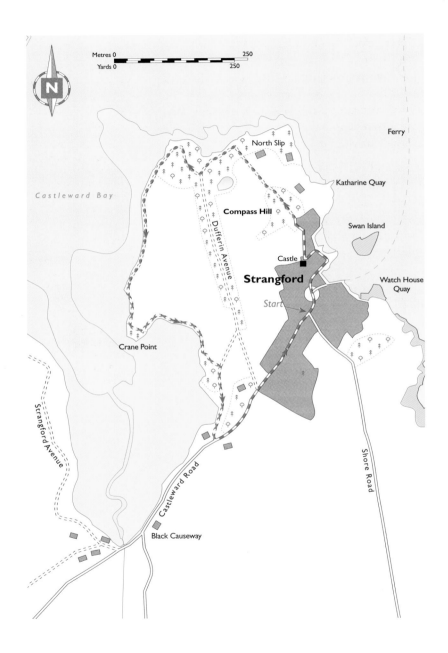

Metres 0 — 250
Yards 0 — 250

N

Ferry

North Slip

Katharine Quay

Castleward Bay

Compass Hill

Swan Island

Dufferin Avenue

Castle

Strangford

Watch House Quay

Start

Crane Point

Strangford Avenue

Castleward Road

Shore Road

Black Causeway

STRANGFORD VILLAGE

Strangford Village Walk extends from the village of Strangford, through a section of Lord de Ros's property, next to the village, and around Strangford Bay. The Royal Society for the Protection of Birds manages an area crossed by the path. The route then returns to the village by a short section of the main Strangford to Downpatrick Road.

Strangford is a small, picturesque village near the entrance to Strangford Lough, opposite the town of Portaferry, situated on the other side of the lough. A passenger and car ferry service which spans this stretch of water, locally known as 'the narrows', links the two settlements.

The Ancient Manor of Strangford came into the ownership of the Earls of Kildare through marriage in the 15th century. Later the Earls of Kildare became the Dukes of Leinster and the 3rd son of the 1st Duke inherited the Manor. He was Lord Henry Fitzgerald. Lord Henry married a lady called Charlotte Boyle-Walshingham who took the de Ros title out of abeyance in the early 19th century, and her descendants still carry the title today.

The walk starts at the square in the centre of the village. Leave the square and walk towards the green next to the harbour area. Follow the road around the green past a newly developed housing scheme on your left. These houses replace the old warehouses that

INFORMATION

Distance: 3.2km (2 miles).

Start and finish: Main square, Strangford.

Terrain: Road, tracks and foreshore. Strong shoes or boots recommended as parts of the walk can be rough and muddy.

Toilets: Ferry terminus.

Refreshments: Wide choice of restaurants, tearooms and pubs in Strangford and Portaferry.

Public transport: Bus service from Downpatrick, car ferry from Portaferry.

Strangford Bay.

stood along the harbour. From the old quays you can observe the car ferry operating and the pleasure and fishing boats moored in the bay.

Swan Island dominates the centre of the harbour. This is a small grass-topped island that is a haven for terns, which return each spring to avail themselves of the rich feeding waters of the narrows. Follow the road around the housing development, then turn left and uphill into Quay Lane.

Strangford.

Towards the top and on the left is Strangford Castle, a 16th century castle built by the Earls of Kildare. The castle, or fortified house, was a 'ten pound house' and was probably never lived in. 'Ten pound houses' were built to ensure that landowners could hold on to their lands. The law at that time stated that no one could hold lands unless they owned a house to the value of at least ten pounds. The castle is now managed by the Department of the Environment. A key is available (see board outside the castle) if you wish to explore it more fully.

Turn right into Castle Street and after passing several houses on your right you will have a beautiful panoramic view of the lough and the town of Portaferry. It is worth spending a few minutes watching the boats and how they manage the currents of the narrows. The road ends at the cast-iron entrance gates into the de Ros estate. At this point a narrow entry on your left leads uphill between high stone walls. Locals call this entry 'Squeeze Gut', the name coming from the activities of courting couples.

The path then passes along a deep woodland ravine where the trees of the de Ros estate tower above on each side. The path can be quite muddy during wet weather. At the bottom the path opens onto a bright grass path and leads down to the water's edge with a hedge on one side and grass meadow on the other.

At the bottom you reach the main estate track, located just above the shore line; turn left at this point.

This area includes several stone wells, called Sarah's Wells, and a purpose-built bathing house and pool. The entrance to this area is marked with a small wooden gate.

Continue walking along the main path as it moves away from the shore, then turn sharp right and follow the sign for Strangford Bay Path. When you reach the shore, turn left and continue along the top of the foreshore. The path takes you around a section of the perimeter of Strangford Bay. On the opposite side is the wooded Castle Ward estate, where you can see the old farmyard and above the trees, Castle Ward House. This section of the walk is rough and can be muddy. The bay nearly dries out at low water, exposing mud flats. The area is always full of wildlife and is very important for feeding birds, especially in the winter months. The RSPB manages part of the bay.

As you approach a small headland with a plantation of trees, Crangs Point, you will be directed away from the foreshore. Climb over a stile, cutting off the headland, and then another to rejoin the foreshore on the other side. Follow the shoreline around another bay until the path veers away from the shore. Climb over a stile and walk along the path until, after another stile, you again join the main estate track. At the track turn right and

continue to a gateway, where you join the main Strangford to Downpatrick Road.

Portaferry from Strangford Quay across the Narrows.

At the road, cross over on to the footpath and turn left towards the village. The entrance to the village is quite charming with a church and picturesque houses and gardens. When you reach the church, cross over on to the next footpath and continue over the hill down to the main square where the walk started.

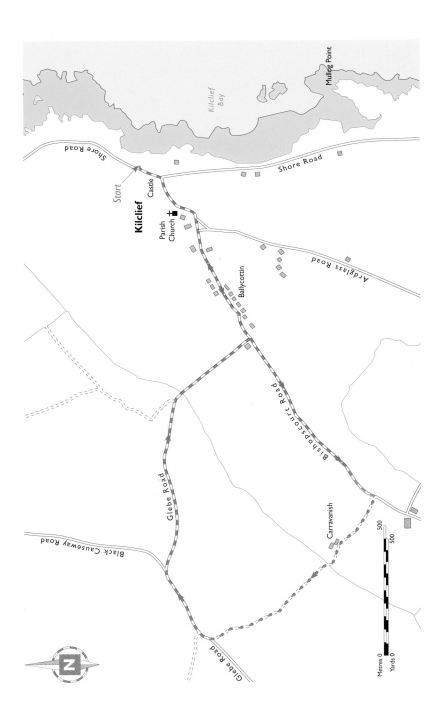

Mullog Point

Kilclief
Bay

Shore Road

Shore Road

Start

Castle

Kilclief

Parish
Church

Ardglass Road

Ballycottin

Bishopscourt Road

Glebe Road

Carravanish

Black Causeway Road

Glebe Road

Metres 0   500
Yards 0   500

KILCLIEF/GLEBE

Kilclief/Glebe Countryside Walk is part public right of way, through rich agriculture land, and part highway along quiet country roads. The walk extends from the shores of Strangford Lough, inland through the small village of Kilclief, and the town lands of Bishopscourt and Ballycottin.

This area of Down District lies in the barony of Lecale, formed by a collection of parishes on the eastern side of County Down. The area is noted for its landscape and today forms part of the Lecale Area of Outstanding Natural Beauty. History has left its mark in the shape of a castle and a nearby motte. The complete area forms the centre of a community that belongs to the ancient parish of Kilclief.

Start the walk at a small informal layby, just above a beautiful sandy beach next to Kilclief Castle. Leave the layby and turn left on to the Shore Road. Cross over to Kilclief Castle, a Watch Tower dating from the 12th century. This is one of many on the shores of Strangford Lough. Ordnance Survey records state that a Bishop of Down inhabited the Castle early in the 15th century. A key is available (see board outside the castle) if you wish to explore it more fully.

INFORMATION

Distance: 5km (3 miles).

Start and finish: Car park and picnic site opposite Kilclief Castle on the A2 Strangford to Ardglass road, 6 km south of Strangford.

Terrain: Road, tracks and paths. Strong shoes or boots recommended as parts of the walk can be uneven and muddy.

Toilets: At the ferry terminal in Strangford.

Refreshments: None on route. Good choice in Strangford; pub in Ballyhornan.

Public transport: Bus service from Downpatrick and Strangford.

Kilclief Castle seen from the carpark/picnic area at Kilclief Beach.

Continue past the castle, keeping to the right, then at the next junction fork right on the Bishopscourt road. This takes you uphill and away from the shore past St Nicholas's Church on your right. This small Church of Ireland church and graveyard is worth a look around. The architecture is simple, yet the church tower is quite a distinctive landmark in the area. From the graveyard the view of Rock Angus Lighthouse, Ballyquintin point on the Ards Peninsula and the entrance to Strangford Lough is striking and unforgettable, especially on a rough day.

Continue past the next junction, still keeping to the right. The road then takes you through the small village of Kilclief which is a mixture of new bungalows, an old school house and public housing estates. After leaving the village the route leads into the countryside and past the Glebe Road junction. The word 'Glebe' comes from the term 'Glebe land', which was land that belonged to the local Church of Ireland clergy. These lands raised income for the local clergyman and the parish.

Rock Angus Lighthouse and entrance to Strangford Lough from Kilclief Beach.

Further along this road a signpost shows a public footpath on your right. Take this path, up a farm lane, towards a small group of farm outhouses at Carravanish. Climb over a stile at the side of a farm gate next to the first building. Continue straight ahead past the next building to another farm gate. Climb over a second stile, at the side of the gate, into a tree-lined and grass-surfaced lane.

This is a very old group of buildings, originally part of some houses belonging to several families, now partly in ruins and used as farm buildings. This is a typical feature of the modern countryside where families have died out, moved on to more modern dwellings, or into the towns for greater convenience or work.

Walk downhill to the bottom of the lane, over yet another stile, into a field. No formal path exists from the stile; just follow the line of the hedgerow that divides the fields. Keep to the side of the ditch and uphill as suggested by the waymark on the side of the stile. On this section of the walk you are in the heart of the countryside. Take time to admire the beautiful views. In the distance and to your left you can see the Mourne Mountains, while all around you observe the small hills or drumlins, farms and small dwelling that make up the County Down landscape.

At the top, cross into the field on your right and climb over a rather high ladder stile into the next field. Again follow the hedge line, this time

Wooden stile giving access to the lane that leads to Glebe Road.

downhill to the bottom of the field. Climb over a wooden stile beside a farm gate. Follow the waymark sign which directs you uphill and across the centre of an open field. Again there is no formal path. As you reach the top of the hill you will see straight ahead a stile in a wooden fence.

Climb over the stile which takes you into a narrow lane. Walk along the lane, which will eventually lead you downhill and over another stile on to the Glebe Road. Turn right at this point and walk along the road, keeping to the right past several road junctions. The road eventually leads you back to the Bishopscourt Road. Turn left when you reach it and walk back through Kilclief Village, downhill past the church and castle, to the small car park where the walk began.

After finishing the walk, if the weather is still pleasant, take a stroll on to the small picturesque beach below the car park. Locals highly recommend a paddle in the waters of Strangford Lough. Good for keeping those feet in shape for your next walk.

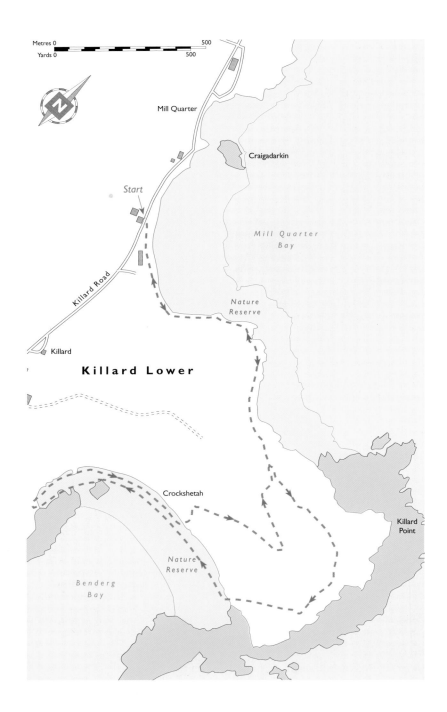

Metres 0   500
Yards 0   500

N

Mill Quarter

Craigadarkin

Start

Mill Quarter Bay

Killard Road

Nature Reserve

Killard

Killard Lower

Crockshetah

Killard Point

Nature Reserve

Benderg Bay

KILLARD NATURE RESERVE

Killard Nature Reserve is at Killard Point, a headland situated on the east coast of Down District at the entrance to Strangford Lough. The area includes the adjoining sandy beach and cliffs at Benderg Bay. The Environment and Heritage Service, an agency within the Department of the Environment, owns and manages the reserve, which is on the coast road between the villages of Strangford and Ballyhornan.

The reserve has a chequered history. Legend states that St Patrick preached to the fishes here in 432 AD. Over the years, people have used it for many purposes. This included managing the area as a rabbit warren and using it for common grazing. A section of the Reserve was used as a hurling pitch for the local Gaelic Club until 1932. Later, the main use of the flat-topped headland was as an RAF radar station from 1952 to 1978.

From the headland you have beautiful views across the entrance to the Lough, where you can see Rock Angus with its lighthouse and various navigation beacons. In the background is the low-lying rocky Ballyquintin Point on the Ards Peninsula. On a clear day, to the seaward side, you get an excellent view of the Isle of Man. Inland, the views of Strangford Lough, the Lecale landscape and the Mourne Mountains show the countryside of Northern Ireland at its best.

INFORMATION

Distance: 5.7km (3.5 miles).

Start and finish: At the side of Killard Road, which is off the main A2 Strangford-Ardglass Road, 2km south of Kilclief Castle and 3.5km north of Ballyhornan.

Terrain: Tracks, foreshore and sand. Strong shoes or boots recommended as the foreshore can be rough and muddy.

Toilets: Ballyhornan or Strangford.

Refreshments: Pub in Ballyhornan. Wider choice in Strangford.

Public transport: Bus service from Downpatrick and Strangford. Car ferry from Portaferry to Strangford.

Opening hours: The reserve is open all year, free. Take time to stop at the car park for Cloughy Rocks Nature Reserve and view the common seals on the rocks offshore. The reserve lies on the seaward side of the A2, just south of Strangford. Further information, tel 01396 615520.

Entrance to Killard Nature Reserve.

Abundant grassland flowers colour the landscape right through the seasons. In spring the pale blue of the spring squill covers the banks. In early summer, the yellow buttercup, kidney vetch, and wild pansies predominate. In July, orchids flower, and in August the purples of knapweed and thyme complete a colourful year.

Start the walk at the entrance off the Killard Road at the northern end of the reserve. The entrance is not easy to find, but if travelling from Kilclief Castle towards Ballyhornan, it is just past the second lay-by on your left. An Environment and Heritage Service signpost, on a grass bank above the foreshore, indicates the reserve boundary. Park your car at this point and walk down the grass bank towards the lough shore. Turn right and, depending on the height of the tide, walk along the beach or foreshore. Remember to take note of the state of the tide for your return journey. A lectern sign just past the row of former Coastguard Cottages gives details of the Reserve.

Ben Derg.

As you round the small bay, you will see eroding sandy banks on your right heavily punched with holes. These are home for the many sand martins which arrive in summer. Continue around these banks until you reach some low-lying grass banks. Leave the beach at this point and step up on to the grass bank. Walk along a narrow grass track that takes you towards Killard Point, the most easterly point of the reserve. As you walk along this stretch, you have excellent views of the narrows, the lighthouse and the entrance to the lough.

Follow the grass tracks along the top of the rocky foreshore. As you reach the point itself, your eye will catch a large beacon on a rock situated about 200m offshore. Locals called the rock after the patron saint of Ireland, St Patrick, and it is now so named officially on Admiralty Charts. When making his first visit to Ireland, the Saint's boat was heading straight for the rock. He held out his staff and touched the rock, which split in two and let the Saint sail safely through.

Continue to walk along the dune and grassland that run along the base of the higher central plateau. When you reach the southern side of the headland, leave the established track and walk towards the sea. Here you will find one of the loveliest sandy beaches in County Down. Walk along the beach of Benderg Bay. The bay, enclosed by rocks on either side, is crescent shaped, faces due south and is a wonderful sun-trap. The high plateau that runs east to west across the reserve forms steep cliffs above the beach. As you near the centre of the bay you will notice the cliff face riddled with holes. These are the homes of sand martins and fulmars and on one visit I saw a fox, probably raiding the cliff for eggs.

After you reach the end of the sandy beach, walk back to where the cliffs started. At the edge of the cliffs, climb up the steep grass bank to the top of the plateau. Then walk along the top towards the easterly point of the escarpment. Again, the views from this section of the walk are quite stunning. The scenery is unforgettable, either by looking out to sea, or inland across the farmland, towards the Mournes, or northwards up Strangford Lough. The small, square buildings on the plateau are relics of the RAF radar station. Now they provide rest-sites for swallows.

Walk around the end of the embankment to the northern face. As you walk along the top of the northern face of the banks, you will observe several small grassy tracks leading down to the bottom. Take any one that will bring you down to join the main track along the top of the foreshore. Turn left when you reach the bottom track, then follow this path back along the top of the foreshore, around the bay and up the grass bank to where the walk started.

Killard Nature Reserve.

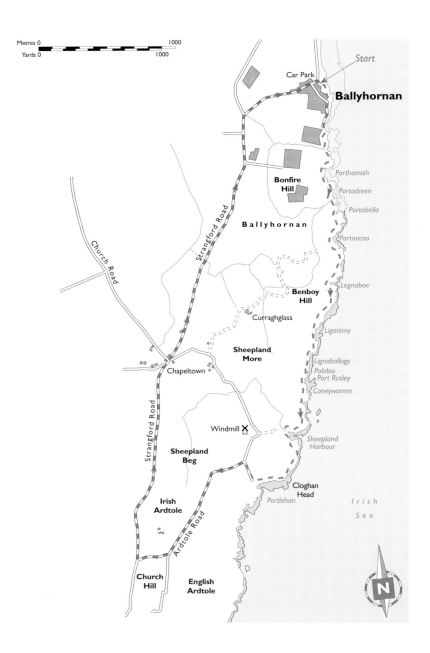

Metres 0   1000
Yards 0   1000

Car Park

Start

Ballyhornan

Porthamish

Portadreen

Portabella

Strangford Road

Bonfire Hill

B a l l y h o r n a n

Portnacoo

Church Road

Legnaboe

Benboy Hill

Curraghglass

Ligatinny

Sheepland More

Lignaballogy

Polidoo

Port Rusley

Chapeltown

Coneywarren

Strangford Road

Windmill

Sheepland Harbour

Sheepland Beg

Cloghan Head

Portlehan

I r i s h

S e a

Irish Ardtole

Ardtole Road

Church Hill

English Ardtole

N

BALLYHORNAN COASTAL PATH

Ballyhornan Coastal Path is situated on the Irish Sea coast, midway between Strangford and Ardglass. It is made up of a public right of way that runs along the cliffs and foreshore between the village of Ballyhornan and Sheepland Road, which is 5km north of the town of Ardglass. This section of the walk forms part of the Ulster Way. From Sheepland the walk continues to Ardtole, along a narrow country road, then joins the Strangford Road (A2) to return, via Chapeltown, to Ballyhornan.

The complete area is within the Baronary of Lecale and the Lecale Area of Outstanding Natural Beauty. The Irish sea and scenic Gun's Island flank the walk on one side, while on the other the picturesque low-lying farmland provides a beautiful backdrop. The area is rich in wildlife, with sea birds in abundance, along the cliff tops and the waters below. On sunny breathless days or in raging gales the area is well worth a visit. Wild flora cover the cliff tops and foreshore, especially in early summer.

The village of Ballyhornan, situated just off the main Strangford to Ardglass Road (A2), is a small community originally made up of fishermen's cottages and farmhouses. In later years, people from Belfast took most of the houses as holiday homes. Most of the local population left the area for work and the convenience of living in larger towns. An RAF base close by at Bishopscourt spilt over into the area. This has now

INFORMATION

Distance: 9.6km (6 miles).

Start and finish: Car park and picnic site on Killard Road at the northern edge of Ballyhornan village.

Terrain: Road, tracks and paths including foreshore. Strong shoes or boots recommended as parts of the walk can be muddy and uneven.

Toilets: In Ballyhornan village.

Refreshments: Pubs in Ballyhornan and Chapeltown; tearoom at Sheepland Farm. Wider choice in Strangford and Ardglass.

Public transport: Bus service from Downpatrick and Strangford.

Opening hours: Sheepland Farm open all year, except Dec. and Jan., from 12 noon to 5pm. Admission charge. Pubs, shops and restaurants normal hours..

Wild flowers on the rocky foreshore.

Path to St Patrick's Well.

closed, and the buildings have been mainly taken over as residential and holiday homes. Although the area is still quiet, people are moving back to live in the village.

The area's main income in years gone by would have been from fishing and farming. A full-time Coastguard Station was based close to the village. Gun's Island, accessible at low tides by wading through the water, would have been very much part of the community. However, the beautiful sandy beach is today as it was always, a favourite place for locals and visitors.

The walk starts on Killard Road, at a car park, just north of the village centre. The car park forms part of a picnic area that runs down to the beach below and is managed by Down District Council. From the car park, walk down a central path and steps towards the sea then turn right along the foreshore. A short path will take you up a grass bank and through an opening in a stone wall on to Rocks Road. Turn left at this point and continue along the narrow road past several small slips, sandy coves, houses and cottages until it stops at the foreshore. A small anchorage for boats lies offshore but because of the exposed nature of the coast, safe anchorage is limited.

Walk along the foreshore and around a small bay, then join another path that leads around the old Coastguard Station, now in ruins. The path continues along grass tracks, up and along cliff tops until you reach a small group of houses called Sheepland. This was a small fishing community with its own natural harbour formed by a narrow inlet between the rocks. Although no official records give any evidence of smuggling, its involvement in this industry is part of folklore. Its isolated location, hidden even from the seaward side, would lead you to believe such stories.

Stay on the foreshore and cross a small burn that flows through the centre of the settlement. Then continue walking in a southerly direction along the grass banks and rocky outcrops above the foreshore. As you round the final headland, the path takes you past a holy shrine that marks St Patrick's Well. Obviously named after the patron saint, the water from the well is supposed to have healing qualities. A few metres past the well, a waymark post points up a farm lane and away from the sea. Walk up this lane and through a gate at the top, bringing you onto the Sheepland Road.

On your right you will notice the ruin of an old mill. This is a well-known landmark that marks the Sheepland area. Turn left and walk towards Ardglass. Keep right at a fork (the Sheepland road) and pass the ruin of St Nicholas Church at Ardtole.

When the road reaches the Strangford Road, turn right towards the small village of Chapeltown. This is a busier road but is still suitable for walking. When you reach Chapeltown, take time to view the chapel and adjoining graveyard or visit a local hostelry. Both will give you a flavour of the community's past and present.

Don't dwell on the flavour too long, however, and take the opportunity to visit Sheepland Farm, a short distance from the centre of the village. This has a small visitor centre designed to illustrate farming of the past. The farm has a tearoom and shop and is pleasant to visit.

Coastal path.

From Chapeltown, continue along the Strangford Road until a sign directs you on to the Killard Road and back to the village of Ballyhornan. Walk through the village back to the car park where the walk began.

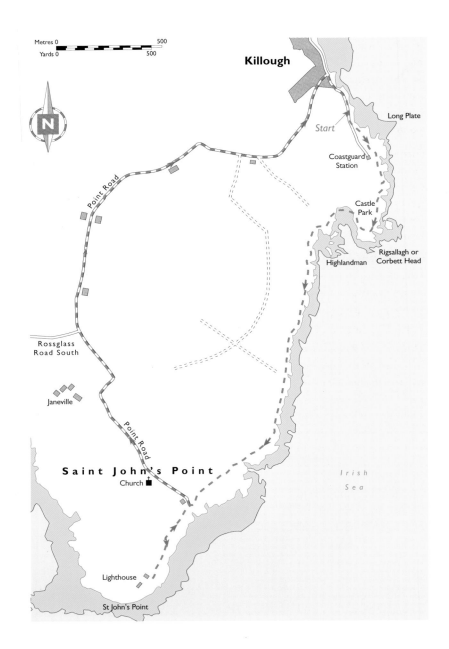

Metres 0   500
Yards 0   500

N

Killough

Start

Long Plate

Point Road

Coastguard
Station

Castle
Park

Highlandman

Rigsallagh or
Corbett Head

Rossglass
Road South

Janeville

Point Road

Saint John's Point
Church

*Irish
Sea*

Lighthouse

St John's Point

KILLOUGH COASTAL PATH

Killough Coastal Path is a public right of way that stretches along the rocky eastern coastline of County Down, on the Irish Sea. The walk runs from Killough village south to St John's Point then returns inland by virtually traffic-free country roads back to the village.

This area of Lecale, in Down District, is less well known because of its isolation away from any public highway or centre of activity. However, it does form a very important section of the Lecale Area of Outstanding Natural Beauty. It is also popular with ornithologists for the number of seabirds and with fishermen who fish off its rocky shores.

Killough village and port, now quiet, were the creation of Michael Ward of Castle Ward, father of the first Lord Bangor. He renamed it Port St Anne, in honour of his wife, and improved the harbour facilities between 1822 and 1824. The village prospered, due to the increased growing of cereals in Lecale. The grain merchants built their imposing houses in the tree-lined Castle Street, giving it a continental flavour. Grain stores dominate the narrow lanes leading to the shore and quays. In the early 19th century, Killough was one of the busiest and most attractive seaside villages in east Down.

The village was also famous for its seafaring past and boasted one of the biggest fishing fleets on the coast. Fishermans Row, a line of cottages on the southern side of the village, would confirm this. Records show

INFORMATION

Distance: 6.4 km (4 miles).

Start and finish: Scordin car park and picnic site, south of Killough village (do not take your car past this point).

Terrain: Road, tracks and paths including foreshore. Strong shoes or boots recommended.

Toilets: In Killough village, near the harbour.

Refreshments: Shops, pubs and restaurants in Killough.

Public transport: Bus service from Downpatrick.

Scordin car park, Killough.

that in 1886 about 50 families were engaged in the trade. Most of the men folk spent the winter months at sea in merchant vessels, travelling widely.

Post-war depression of the 1930s brought a fall in grain prices, leading to the closing of grain stores and to the harbour lying idle. The closure of the railway in 1950 and the erratic opening and eventual closing of the brickworks have meant the village is mainly now residential.

In recent years Down District Council has restored the harbour, and although no significant increase in usage happened, the opportunity for development now exists. New public housing and the number of private houses built, with improvements to property, along the tree-lined Castle Street, are breathing new life into the village.

The walk starts at the southern end of the village, at Scordin car park and picnic site, just opposite the Coastguard Rescue Station. Turn left when you leave the car park and walk towards the former Coastguard Station. At the bottom of the hill a signpost directs you off the tarmac road on to a public path. This is a grass track that heads seaward along a fence. Climb over the stile provided and go straight ahead along the grassy banks at the top of the rocky foreshore.

This will take you around the perimeter of a large field called the Park Field. Waymarked posts lead you down a steep bank on to the foreshore that lies below clay cliffs. The path then leads you back off the beach up a steep bank and on to grass-topped rocky promontories.

Again you are directed on to the beach, and depending on the height of the tide, across a small bay to a small ladder-stile on the other side. Climb up the ladder and onto a grass track that leads you over more grass and rocky outcrops. The next section of the walk can be quite muddy and wet underfoot; however, some stepping stones and a little dainty footwork will get you through.

A little further on, step over another stile which takes you over a fence line. A waymark post directs you uphill, away from the shore to another stile. After climbing this stile, turn left and return to the grass banks above the foreshore. From here it is quite straightforward; head towards St John's Point Lighthouse, climb over a couple of stiles, and keep parallel to the fields on the upper side of the walk. Finally climb over a stile beside a pillar and on to the Point Road.

When you reach this point it is worth taking a short diversion to visit St John's Point Lighthouse. The lighthouse, perched on a rocky headland, on which many ships were wrecked, guards one of the busiest shippings lanes of the Irish Sea. Large ships and fishing boats use it as an important landmark when trying to avoid the hazards of Dundrum Bay and the rocky coasts of Down. After much pressure from merchants and shipowners the Dublin Ballast Board (later the Commissioners of Irish Lights) built it with a foghorn in 1844. In 1893 they raised the height of the lighthouse, and built houses for the lightkeepers and their families. The light was electrified in 1980 and it is now fully automatic, although retaining some manual cover.

St John's Point Lighthouse.

After returning to the point where you joined the road, continue past a cottage and uphill away from the lighthouse towards the ruins of St John's church, which are cared for by the Department of the Environment.

Continue uphill past a large farmhouse (Janeville) on your left, then past the junction with the Rossglass Road South, and back towards the village of Killough. Stay with this road, which passes through well-farmed agricultural land. After you enter the village and reach the shore, turn right. This will take you back to the car park at Scordin where the walk started.

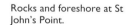

Rocks and foreshore at St John's Point.

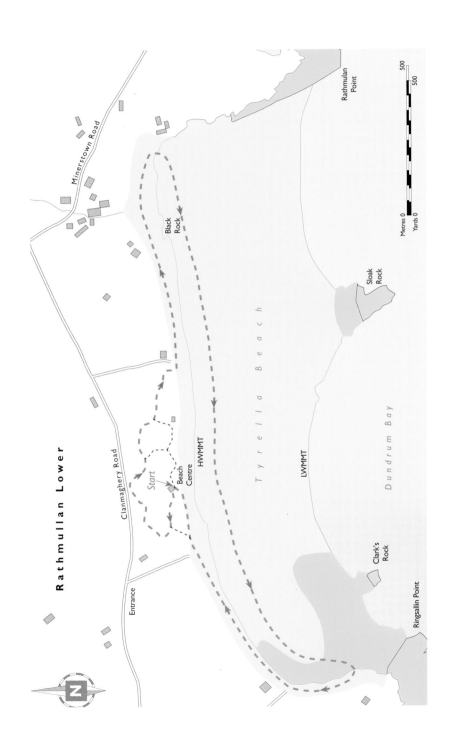

Rathmullan Lower

Minerstown Road

Clanmaghery Road

Entrance

Start

Beach Centre

Black Rock

HWMMT

LWMMT

Tyrella Beach

Dundrum Bay

Sloak Rock

Clark's Rock

Ringsallin Point

Rathmullan Point

Metres 0   500
Yards 0   500

TYRELLA BEACH

Tyrella Beach is a small enclosed beach and dune complex on the shores of Dundrum Bay on the Irish Sea coast. It is within the Lecale Area of Outstanding Natural Beauty and consists of a wide sandy beach, backed by a mature dune area and agricultural land.

The Countryside Development Section of Down District Council now own and manage the central section of the beach. This is a wide sandy area 2 km long, backed by 25 hectares of mature dune conservation area.

A fall in sea level probably formed the dunes after 6,500 BC, allowing blown sand to accumulate above the high-water mark. Controlling access to the dunes has conserved its flora and fauna so visitors can continue to enjoy this valuable natural resource. The Council can arrange private guided walks for groups and educational establishments.

Tyrella Beach is the top public beach in Down District and provides a safe and clean environment for swimmers and people enjoying healthy recreation. The Council manages the beach to European Blue Flag standards with special car-free zones and a modern Beach Centre.

Begin the walk at the Beach Centre, which is in the centre of the car-free zone at the top of the beach. Before starting, it is worth having a look at the exhibition in the centre. The display describes the conservation programme for the dune area and the history of the beach as a recreation area.

INFORMATION

Distance: 4km (2.5 miles).

Start and finish: Tyrella, on the coast road between Killough and Clough, 11 km from Downpatrick and 8 km from Newcastle.

Terrain: Paths and foreshore. Strong shoes recommended.

Toilets: At the Beach Centre.

Refreshments: Seasonal cafe.

Opening hours: The beach is open every day of the year. The Beach Centre is open during the summer season only (subject to weather). Pubs, shops and restaurants normal hours.

NOTE: No public transport passes the beach.

Dunes with St John's Point in the distance.

Leave the Beach Centre area by taking the path at the rear of the premises that heads west towards the entrance. After passing through a wooden kissing gate, follow a path constructed of a timber boardwalk bedded into the sand. All the paths follow a natural track in the dunes. Vegetation is gradually re-establishing itself on the path, which helps protect against further sand erosion.

One of the walkways through the dune area.

Continue past the junction with a path on your left and veer right as the path heads away from the beach. This gives you a good opportunity to observe the dune formation and vegetation behind the beach. The path then takes you in an easterly direction and heads close to the main road. As you approach the road, the path makes a 90-degree turn back towards the sea. The board walk disappears at this stage and netting stretched across the path protects the route.

Follow the path as it veers left. A short distance later you will arrive at a fork. Walk straight ahead, ignoring the path that turns to your right. This will eventually lead you to the main conservation area. Another fork in the path appears just before you enter a fenced-off area. Again, ignore the route to your right and continue straight ahead. These forks are short cuts that will eventually lead you back to the beach centre. The fenced area protects a section of the conservation area that contains wild orchids and other rare species of flora. Continue along the path until it eventually swings right, then through a wooden kissing gate and onto the beach. Turn left at this point and head east towards St John's Point Lighthouse.

This famous lighthouse marks the northern boundary of Dundrum Bay, infamous for the number of shipwrecks that occurred during the days of sailing vessels. Dundrum Bay's half-moon shape and an onshore wind made it very difficult for ships travelling along the coast. Ships found it almost impossible to get off a lee shore during gale force winds.

Continue past a small stream near the top boundary of the beach, then turn and walk back towards the Beach Centre. To vary your route, walk along the water's, edge especially if the tide is out. This gives a different perspective of the beach and the dune area behind. As you go back, you will get a magnificent view of the Mourne Mountains above the town of Newcastle.

Walk past the Beach Centre and continue to the south-western boundary of the beach. As you walk, observe the different types of seaweed and shells along the water's edge. Tyrella is more than a beach resort for people on a sunny summer day. You can visit Tyrella for recreation anytime of the year and in all sorts of weather. It is as rewarding on a stormy day in winter as it is during a heat wave in summer. Just be sure to wear the appropriate clothes.

Be careful as you walk over the rocks at the end of the beach, as it can be slippery. Do take time to explore the marine life in the rock pools before turning back to the Beach Centre. Use the top of the beach for your return journey. The sand or gravel can be soft in places making it difficult to walk, however, a keen eye can probably pick the firmer ground.

Several hundred metres further on, you will arrive back at the Beach Centre where the walk began.

The Beach Centre with the Mournes in the distance.

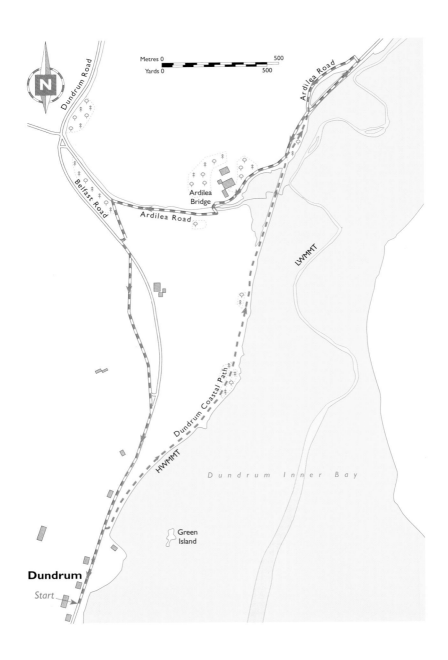

Dundrum Road

Ardilea Road

Metres 0   500
Yards 0   500

Belfast Road

Ardilea Bridge

Ardilea Road

LWMMT

Dundrum Coastal Path

HWMMT

Dundrum Inner Bay

Green Island

Dundrum

Start

DUNDRUM COASTAL WALK

undrum Coastal Walk extends along a disused section of railway line and the public highway. The walk is on the shores of Dundrum Inner Bay, just north of Dundrum village. The railway section, managed by the National Trust, forms a unique nature reserve for wild flora and fauna overlooking the mudflats that form the Inner Bay.

Beyond the mudflats, on the other side of the bay, is the Army base at Ballykinler. The base is on a dune system similar to Murlough Nature Reserve (Walk 14), found on the opposite side of the estuary that connects the bay to the Irish Sea.

Dundrum Bay is internationally important as a wintering area for seabirds. The outer bay stretches from St John's Point in the north-east to the Mourne Mountains in the south-west, backed by the dune systems of Murlough and Ballykinler. The Inner Bay is a tidal lagoon, fed by several small rivers, connected to the sea by a narrow channel. It is the supply of fish, in particular sand eels and herring, which makes Dundrum Bay so important as a feeding area for thousands of seabirds.

The village of Dundrum has been associated with the sea and seafaring for many generations. It was until recently the main port for imports of coal and general cargo into the area. The quays remain, and thriving

INFORMATION

Distance: 6.4km (4 miles).

Start and finish: On the Downpatrick road, at the entrance to Dundrum village.

Terrain: Road, path and track. Strong shoes or boots recommended as parts of the walk can be muddy.

Toilets: In Dundrum village.

Refreshments: Good choice in Dundrum.

Public transport: Bus services from Downpatrick and Newcastle.

Dundrum Coastal Walk.

businesses still operate in the harbour area. However, changes in transport have superseded the boats. Transporting goods by road is now cheaper.

The walk starts at the Downpatrick end of the village. Using the footpath, walk along the main road leading out of the village. A few hundred metres later, cross the road at the Ulster Way signpost and take a dirt lane towards the sea. Then take a sharp left before the entrance to a private house. This will guide you onto the old railway track. Once the main route from Belfast to Newcastle, it was closed, like so many others, in the 1950s.

Walk along the track away from the village. The route passes along the shoreline of Dundrum Inner Bay and is a haven for all sorts of wildlife. It is unbelievable how an old railway line can be such an excellent nature reserve. This section is managed by the National Trust, who carry out the minimum of maintenance necessary to prevent it becoming totally wild.

Views from the path are beautiful, especially if you look over your shoulder and observe the Mournes as they sweep down to the sea. Anywhere along the path is excellent for birdwatching. Birdlife includes shelduck, mallard, redbreasted mergansers, herons and moorhen, and if you are lucky you may spot a kingfisher. Seabirds include many different gulls, gannets, cormorants and shags.

The keen naturalist can enjoy the varied vegetation and its inhabitants. Behind the track is open and well-worked fertile farmland typical of this part of County Down, while across the bay are the low-lying fields that eventually merge with the dune area of Ballykinler.

Ardilea Motte.

Two-thirds of the way along the track at Ardilea, it crosses the estuary of a small river that flows from the rich surrounding farmland into the bay. Halfway across you can pause at the first of two bridges and gaze into the water below. You might spot a salmon.

After crossing the estuary, the path nears then runs parallel to the Ardilea road. At this point, the trees on either side form an arch and almost cover the path. A little further on, a brackish pond or lagoon appears on the left. Here the railway has trapped water between itself and the main land. The pond is quite extensive but difficult to access due to the thick vegetation. Being quiet, it is frequented by otters.

Picturesque bay on the Dundrum Coastal Path.

Just before the railway track ends, you pass over another bridge. Go down a small flight of steps which lead you off the track onto the Ardilea Road. Turn left and start walking back towards Dundrum. The road leads back along the other side of the pond, over a small hill, and down to where it rejoins the track.

Stay on the road and it will take you away from the track and along the side of the river estuary. This is a picturesque stretch, passing some elegant farm gates, and over the Ardilea Bridge. Turn right after you cross the bridge and continue along the road which runs parallel to the river bank. Take the first road on the left, climbing a steep hill to the main Downpatrick to Newcastle road. Turn left and after a short distance, cross over and take the 'Old Belfast Road' on the other side. This is a very busy crossing, so please take care.

Start walking up the Dundrum Road, which is much quieter and better suited for walkers, past the old Gate Lodge belonging to Mount Panther House. Continue up the road which climbs a hill and then veers left, down towards the village. The view of the bay and the mountains from this road, and the lack of traffic, make the small diversion worthwhile.

At the end of the road, rejoin the main road. Keep right at this point and take the hard shoulder until you reach the footpath which leads back to Dundrum. The path leads you past the Gaelic football pitch and back into the village.

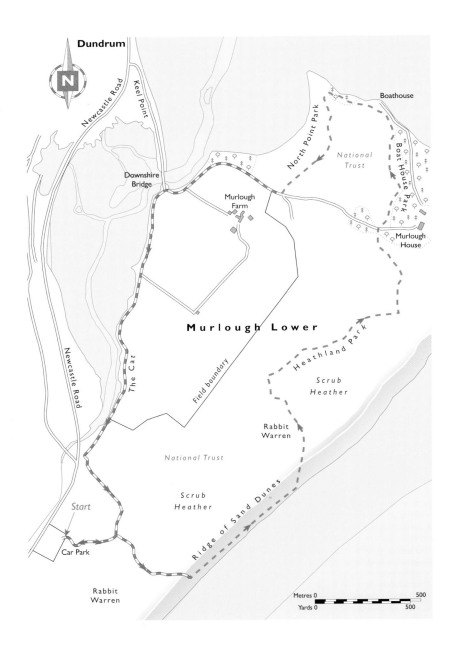

Dundrum

N

Newcastle Road

Keel Point

Downshire
Bridge

Murlough
Farm

North Point Park

Boathouse

Boat House Park

*National
Trust*

Murlough
House

Murlough Lower

Field boundary

Heathland Park

*Scrub
Heather*

Newcastle Road

The Cat

Rabbit
Warren

National Trust

*Scrub
Heather*

Ridge of Sand Dunes

Start

Car Park

Rabbit
Warren

Metres 0   500
Yards 0   500

MURLOUGH NATURE RESERVE

Murlough Nature Reserve is a National Trust property situated on the shores of Dundrum Bay between Dundrum and Newcastle. The Trust acquired it from the Marquess of Downshire's estate, and in 1967 established the area as Ireland's first Nature Reserve. In 1995, the reserve and some surrounding areas were designated as the Murlough Site of Special Scientific Interest. The area also forms part of the Mourne Area of Outstanding Natural Beauty.

Murlough Nature Reserve is approximately 282 hectares in extent and forms part of a sand dune system developed across Dundrum Bay. The area is of great interest to the geographer, naturalist and archaeologist because of its prehistoric formation, the wide range of plants and animals and evidence of early settlements.

Older dunes, some 20-30 m high, are at least 6,000 years old; younger ones nearer the sea soar to 40 m. They support a variety of plant life, including the rare Portland spurge, carline thistle and pyramidal orchid. Murlough contains some fine examples of dune heath, a type of habitat that is rare in Europe.

Begin the walk at the Trust car park and Information Centre near the main entrance. Walk towards the rear of the car park and through a gate at the left-hand side. Turn left, along the fence line, then right at the first fork. Follow this grass path towards a timber surfaced path. Walk along this path until it joins another timber path. Turn right and follow the path towards and between several high dunes which lead to

INFORMATION

Distance: 8 km (5 miles).

Start and finish: National Trust car park, signposted off the A2 road just south of Dundrum. Car park charge in summer only.

Terrain: Boardwalks, estate roads and tracks. No special footwear needed.

Toilets: Main car park, next to the entrance, July-August. Also at the picnic site opposite the pedestrian entrance, all year.

Refreshments: Good choice in Dundrum.

Opening hours: Some footpaths are open all year,m dawn to dusk. Others are only open Oct to end March. A shop/ exhibition area is open July and Aug

Public transport: Bus service from Newcastle and Downpatrick.

Note: Dogs must be kept on leads at all times. No dogs allowed in fenced areas. For further information tel 013967 51467.

Murlough Nature Reserve.

the sea. As you approach the foreshore you will observe a white post. Leave the dune area at this point, walk over the high gravel bank on to the sandy beach, then turn left.

The beach is a beautiful sandy, shell-strewn strand stretching from the seaside town of Newcastle to the estuary that leads into Dundrum Inner Bay.

To your right is the vast expanse of Dundrum Bay, infamous for being a danger to sailing vessels. One of the more famous wrecks was in 1846 when the *Great*

Britain, designed by the renowned British engineer and ship designer I.K.Brunel, ran aground. This was the world's largest iron steam-ship, and is now restored in its home city of Bristol.

Dundrum bay at
Murlough beach.

Turn left at the red-topped post and follow the path back into the dunes. After a short distance you will reach a wooden gate in a fence line. Go through the gate and head towards a yellow waymark post. At the second yellow marker follow the path inland; this path is known as the Archaeological Path. The waymarks are not obvious but follow the tracks and they soon appear. This section of the route is remarkable as it is here you really feel the magnitude of the dunes. The walk climbs uphill one minute then down into a large depression the next. Heathland vegetation is very rich along each side of the path, with lots of grasses interspersed with heather, sea buckthorn, bracken and wild flowers.

As you near the end of this section of the path, you will reach a second area of heather fenced off like a paddock. Turn right before reaching the paddock and walk parallel to the fence. This path, called the Heathland Path, follows the line of a main firebreak. At first it is not very visible but becomes more definitive later when it gently veers to the right, back towards the sea, and then left and up a short steep slope.

Continue until it passes through a timber gate in the fence line. Turn left and stay with the path. It then veers to your left and uphill. The path then swings right and across the tarmac estate road, near Murlough House, on to the Boat House Path.

The path leaves the shore and becomes the 'North Point Path'. It then continues uphill. At the top you get a view of the complete Mourne mountain range. Continue along this path, ignoring a path that branches off to the right, then cross over a bridlepath marked with blue posts. A short distance ahead you will again join the tarmac estate road. Turn right, around a slight bend, and walk down a secluded tree-lined roadway.

The road has a farm and large meadow on your left and a small wooded area on your right. Towards the end of the road you again see the inner bay and a small picturesque bridge. This is the Downshire Bridge; it has three beautiful stone arches and joins the Murlough peninsula to the mainland and the village of Dundrum.

Walk through a gateway and past a delightful stone gate lodge. Follow the road to the right, avoiding the entrance to Murlough Farm. Then take a gravel track that branches to the left and onto a road called The Cut. This extends right

Mournes from Murlough beach.

along the shoreline of the inner bay, back towards Newcastle. This section of the bay is rich in wildlife.

The route passes several cottages and continues until it reaches a pedestrian entrance beside the main Dundrum-Newcastle road. Turn left before you reach the main road. This will take you along the Slidderyford Path back towards the dunes and onto a boardwalk. Continue along the path until you reach another boardwalk that branches to the right. This is the path on which you originally started; follow it back to the information centre and car park where the walk began.

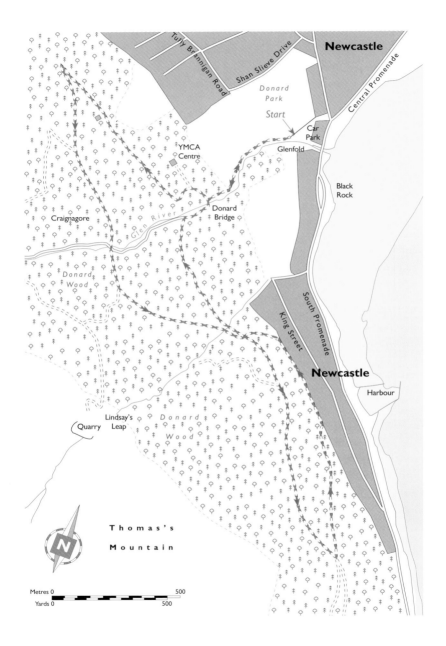

Newcastle

Tully Brannigan Road

Shan Slieve Drive

Central Promenade

Donard Park

Start

Car Park

Glenfold

Black Rock

YMCA Centre

Glen River

Donard Bridge

Craignagore

Donard Wood

South Promenade

King Street

Newcastle

Harbour

Lindsay's Leap

Donard Wood

Quarry

Thomas's Mountain

Metres 0   500

Yards 0   500

DONARD FOREST

Donard Forest is managed by the Department of Agriculture and is situated at the foot of the Mournes on the outskirts of the seaside town of Newcastle. The forest belongs to the Annesley Family and is leased by the Department. It covers an area of 280 hectares and has many viewing points which give spectacular views over the surrounding coastal plains and drumlins.

One of the main features of the forest is the Glen River which runs through the centre of the wood. The river has a series of cascades and waterfalls. A path which runs along its length forms the main access point for walkers to climb Slieve Donard, the highest peak in the Mournes. (Walk 16)

Donard Forest is entered through Donard Park, an amenity park managed by Down District Council. The park contains one of the town's main car parks.

Start the walk by going through the car park and into the open parkland at the rear. Keep to the left until you enter the wood at the top of the park. At this point you will see the Glen River. Follow the river until it reaches Donard Bridge, built in 1835. Upstream of the bridge is an array of picturesque cascades and waterfalls fringed by broadleaved woodland.

To the right of the bridge you will find a map displaying the different routes through the forest.

INFORMATION

Distance: 8 km (5 miles).

Start and finish: Donard Park car park, Newcastle.

Terrain: Forest roads, tracks and paths. Boots or strong shoes recommended. All trails involve sections of steep climbs and descents over rough and uneven ground.

Toilets: At the car park.

Refreshments: Wide choice in Newcastle.

Public transport: Buses from all major towns to Newcastle.

Note: Please take note of hazard warning notices along the Glen River. For further information contact the head forester, tel 013967 78664.

Donard forest.

There are four waymarked trails. This walk follows the Contour Trail, coloured blue on the official map, as it offers the best route for seeing the majority of the forest and its viewing points.

Start by taking the forest road uphill and to the right of the notice board. Pass the entrance to the YMCA centre. Further up the road, the woodland on each side has been removed and young trees planted to ensure a future crop of timber. Once you enter this area, the first of the wider views commence.

Follow the path past a cottage and towards a forest gate. Walk around the gate, used to control vehicular traffic, and continue uphill. A second forest road appears from the left, behind and above the path you have just climbed. Take this road and head back towards the Glen River. Stop wherever you like and enjoy the panoramic view. From here you can look down on the streets, parks and buildings of the town of Newcastle.

Dundrum Bay and Newcastle from Donard Forest.

Keep to this path, ignoring a track uphill to the right, which takes you back into the forest to the Glen River Bridge. The bridge was built by the Annesley family and formed part of the pleasure grounds of the demesne. Above and below the bridge are a series of cascades and waterfalls. Take time to enjoy the scenery and listen to the water gushing over the rocks and boulders.

The path continues through the woodland to a second bridge that spans Amy's River. The route is confusing at his point and the walker could be misled by the presence of another path that heads downhill and back towards the Glen River. Ignore this path and continue straight ahead.

Climb uphill along the path and through the trees. Look out for an opening in the trees that forms a corridor across your path. This was formed by an old railway track used to transport granite from the quarry, high up on the mountain, to the harbour below. This track, or corridor, is known as the 'Bogie Line'.

Dundrum Bay and Newcastle from Donard Forest.

A few hundred metres further on, the path is joined by another track coming from below. Turn at this point and use this path to walk downhill, back towards Newcastle. As the path descends, observe through the trees the harbour below. During the last century, sailing vessels collected dressed granite such as paving-setts, kerbstones and stone for monuments, for use in major cities including Liverpool and Belfast. The boats returned with coal and slate.

Cross the 'Bogie Line' again. The surrounding trees are predominantly Scots pine with a small compartment of beech and European larch. The walk goes right down to the rear of the houses that form the southern end of the town. Do not go to the end of the path as it does not lead anywhere. Instead, leave the path at a point marked with a wooden waymark post.

This is a less formal path which leads up a steep narrow track back to the position at Amy's River where two paths merged. Take the waymarked path from here to the right and downhill. Several hundred metres on you will pass a stone grotto on your left. The grotto, with a central stone table built of natural boulders, formed part of the pleasure grounds of the original demesne.

Continue downhill until the path once again joins the Glen River path. Turn right and walk down the track back to Donard Bridge and the Information Board. From here, retrace your steps to the car park where the walk started.

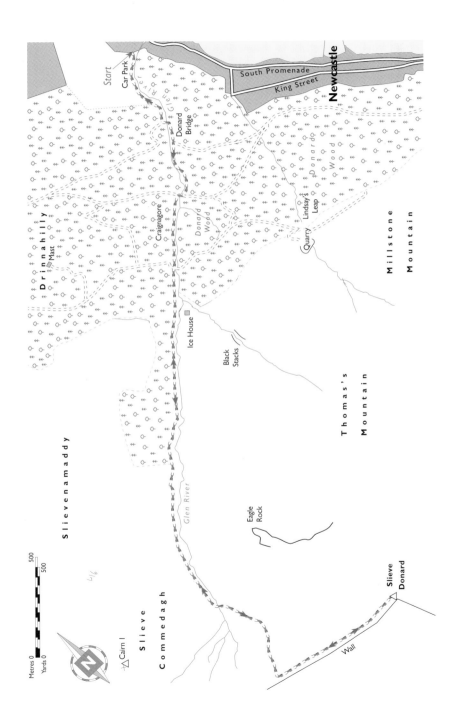

Metres 0 500
Yards 0 500

N

Cairn I

Slievenamaddy

Slieve
Commedagh

Slieve
Donard

Glen River

Eagle
Rock

Wall

Drinnahilly

Mast

Craignagore

Ice House

Black
Stacks

Thomas's
Mountain

Donard
Wood

Quarry

Lindsay's
Leap

Donard
Bridge

Glen River

Donard Wood

Start

Car Park

South Promenade

King Street

Newcastle

Millstone
Mountain

SLIEVE DONARD

This walk extends from Donard Park, Newcastle to the top of Slieve Donard, at 850m the highest peak of the Mourne Mountains. Newcastle is a seaside resort on the shores of Dundrum Bay and is a major gateway to the Mournes and a 'Mecca' for hill and mountain walkers and climbers.

The landscape of the Mournes is essentially romantic. Their fame does not depend on their height, but on their beauty, strength and power. They are viewed from many parts of County Down and best remembered by Irish exiles in Percy French's ballad *The Mountains of Mourne*.

Although the mountain landscape is dominated by heath and boulders, there are many areas of bog and vegetation with sedges, moss and heathers to interest the walker or naturalist. The lower slopes of the mountain are forested, managed by the Department of Agriculture. Although the trees are mainly coniferous, deciduous varieties are gradually being introduced.

A well known feature of the Mournes is the massive granite wall, built between 1910 and 1922 by the Belfast Water Commissioners to define their catchment area. It runs for 35 km over the top of 15 mountains and encloses 3645 hectares.

Birds on the mountain include ravens, kestrels, meadow pipit, skylark all seen at the appropriate times of the year in their respective environments. Walkers can also see the Irish hare and fox on the lower slopes, but the predominant four-legged animals are the sheep that graze every part of the mountain.

The National Trust has now acquired the large northern portion of Donard up to the summit including the whole of the upper Glen River valley. The Trust area includes

INFORMATION

Distance: 9 km (5.5 miles).

Ascent: approx 800m.

Start and finish: Donard Park car park, Newcastle.

Terrain: Tracks and hill paths. Boots essential as much of the walk is over rough or rocky ground. Take food and drink, windproof/waterproof clothing and an Ordnance Survey map. The summit is often in cloud and can be very much colder than it is at sea level.

Toilets: in the car park.

Refreshments: Wide choice in Newcastle.

Further information: Contact the Mourne Information Centre, tel 013967 24059.

Glen river and Eagle rock.

the whole of the mountain landscape above the Donard Lodge plantation.

The Trust, with grant-aid from the Environment and Heritage Service, is tackling the problem of erosion on the Glen River path. Repairing the path with the agreement of Down District Council has been very effective and it can now carry the many thousands of people that use it each year.

Mournes in winter.

The walk begins in Donard Park, the town's main car park. Walk from the rear of the park towards the mountains through a gate and into a public park. A track leads you along the left-hand side of a large open space recreation area. The Glen River runs parallel to this path and just behind a hedge that forms the boundary of the park. At the top left-hand corner, the path enters Donard Wood which is managed by the Forest Service of the Department of Agriculture (Walk 15).

Continue up the path, criss-crossed by the roots of trees, until you reach a bridge on your left. Cross the bridge onto the river's left bank. Note the signs that warn you not to stand close to the river banks. The views from the bridge show the waterfalls and cascades as the river falls 500 m from the granite slopes above.

After a 400m climb the path reaches a second bridge and another chance to observe the cascades and enormous granite outcrops occupying the river bed. Re-cross the river on to its right side and continue upstream. After a further 400m you reach a third bridge. Remain on the right bank and continue until you reach a stile marking the end of the wood on one side and the beginning of the open hillside. Follow the track along the river for a further 2 km.

One item to note is an igloo-like stone building on the opposite side of the river. This was an 'ice house' built by the Annesley family, and was their refrigerator, used to store ice and game for their kitchens. The National Trust is now restoring the building, which has suffered from the attention of inquisitive visitors over the years. Just below the ice house a tributary joins the Glen River after cascading down a dark rocky cleft, known as 'The Black Stairs', on the side of nearby Thomas's Mountain.

As the track ascends the valley, the prominent scree-fringed buttress of Eagle Rock overlooks the far bank of the river. On the right is Slieve Commedagh and the vast corrie known as the Pot of Pulgarve. Further ahead, at a narrow point, cross the river and continue uphill. The path then rises quite steeply to reach the 'Saddle' and the Mourne Wall. From this point you can walk to the top of Slieve Donard, by following the Mourne Wall, uphill to the summit. This section is particularly strenuous.

Walkers on the path above Glen River.

Slieve Donard is the main feature of the Down District landscape. Legend states that the peak was named after St Domangard, a local chieftain who became a disciple of St Patrick. A stone cairn on the summit is believed to be a prayer cell.

While on the mountain it is worth a visit to Slieve Commedagh, which offers a different view over the Annalong valley and the complete range of Mourne peaks. To complete the walk, retrace your steps down the mountain and the Glen River to Donard Park car park where the walk started.

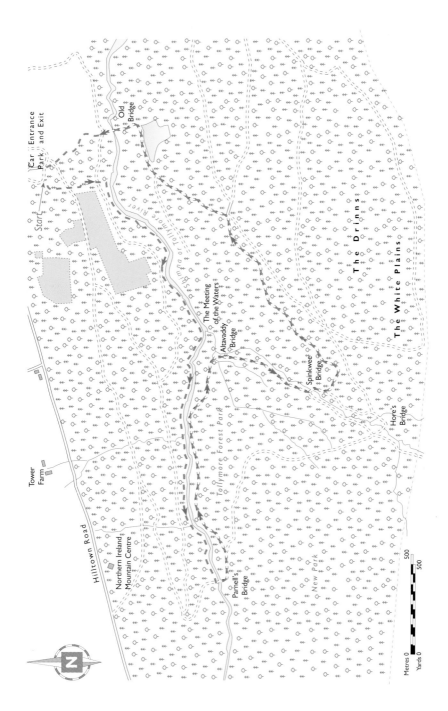

Car Entrance
Park and Exit

Start

Old
Bridge

Bassmpa or Tollymore River

The Meeting
of the Waters

Altavaddy
Bridge

The Drins

The White Plains

Spinkwee
Bridge

Hore's
Bridge

Tower
Farm

Northern Ireland
Mountain Centre

Hilltown Road

Tollymore Forest Park

Parnell's
Bridge

New Park

Metres 0

Yards 0

500

500

TOLLYMORE FOREST PARK

Tollymore Forest Park is a Department of Agriculture property situated near the village of Bryansford. The property was previously owned by Robert Jocelyn, 8th Earl of Roden. It was the first State Forest in Northern Ireland to be designated as a Forest Park. Covering an area of almost 500 hectares, the park lies at the foot of the Mourne Mountains, and provides panoramic views of the mountains and the Irish Sea coast that forms Dundrum Bay.

The main feature of the park is the Shimna River, which flows along a rocky bed through the centre of the park from the Mournes to the sea at Newcastle. The tree-shaded river with its numerous deep pools is home to a variety of birds and mammals such as dippers, kingfishers and otters.

Various stone bridges cross the river. These ornate bridges, some of which were constructed over 200 years ago by various owners of the estate, are fine examples of the stonemason's craft. Several of them were built in honour or in remembrance of relatives and friends. Another feature is a series of Forest Plots and an Arboretum. The Barbican Gate forms the main entrance to the Forest Park and is striking because of the cedar-lined avenue.

There are four waymarked trails of varying lengths within the park. All follow a circular route and are signposted from the information board in the main car park.

INFORMATION

Distance: 5 km (3 miles).

Start and finish: Main car park, Tollymore, signposted from both the A50 and the A2.

Terrain: Paths and tracks. Strong shoes or boots recommended.

Toilets: Several within the park, including at the main car park.

Refreshments: Restaurant adjacent to main car park (Mar-Oct). Tearoom near main entrance. Wider choice in Castlewellan and Newcastle.

Public transport: Bus service from Newcastle.

Opening hours: Grounds open all year, 10.00-dusk. Admission charge. Further information, tel 01396 778664.

Stepping stones on the Shimna River.

The Hermitage.

The Rivers Trail, perhaps the most picturesque and interesting, is described here. Others are well worth trying, especially the Long Haul Trail which requires a higher degree of stamina, but does enter the more remote areas of the forest.

The walk starts at the information panel in the main car park and follows blue waymarks. Begin by descending the Azalea Walk, a delightful stroll downhill through a stone sculptured ravine.

At the bottom you enter the wood and are directed to a path which runs along the northern banks of the Shimna River. From here you follow the river upstream. The quick-flowing and tree-lined river is absolutely beautiful and the sound of water rushing over the boulders can at times smother all other noises. The forest is so dense in places it that it gets really dark. Openings in the forest canopy over the river provide a unique contrast of light and colour. This makes the walk visually impressive and an artist's and photographer's paradise.

As you follow the stream you are directed to a stone structure called the Hermitage, built by James Hamilton, Second Earl of Clanbrassil, as a memorial to a friend, the Marquis of Monthermer, who died in 1770.

Moving on from this point, the wood opens into an area where some clearance and replanting has been carried out by the Forestry Service. Continue along the route and you return to mature woodland and the first of some stepping stones across the river. This is just below a point called the 'meeting of the waters' where the Shimna is joined by the Spinkwee River. The stepping stones form part of a weir, are man made, and can be used to cross the river.

Further upstream you will reach the Rustic Bridge. This is a picturesque timber bridge used by many visitors for taking photographs - and of course crossing the river.

Continue past the bridge and walk along the river bank until you reach the second and third set of stepping stones.

A short distance later you will arrive at Parnell's Bridge, named after Sir John Parnell, who was at one time Chancellor of the Exchequer in Ireland, and the great-grandfather of the famous Irish politician C. S. Parnell. This marks the westerly limit of the walk. After crossing the river, turn left and head downstream. You will again pass the stepping stones and the Rustic Bridge, only on the opposite side.

Parnell's Bridge.

Continue until you approach Altavaddy Bridge. Turn right before the bridge and walk uphill, away from the Shimna River and along the fast-flowing Spinkwee River. This is quite a steep climb after the previous riverside walk, but should be within everyone's capabilities. As you walk up to Spinkwee Bridge, take time to leave the path and view the Cascade Falls from the wooden platforms provided. This 10 m cascade of water is one of the most spectacular features of Tollymore.

After crossing the bridge, climb uphill again, following the waymark signs. These lead you on to one of the main forestry roads through tall fir and larch trees and eventually back down towards the Lake. Here you can rest and observe the colourful ducks and wildfowl.

From the lake, continue the walk back to the Shimna River and the Old Bridge. After crossing the bridge, leave the shaded banks of the Shimna to climb the steep grass covered slopes of the Green Rig to the car park where the walk began. The last leg up this slope is particularly strenuous. You will be glad to rest on the seats at the top and enjoy the marvellous views across the forest and beyond.

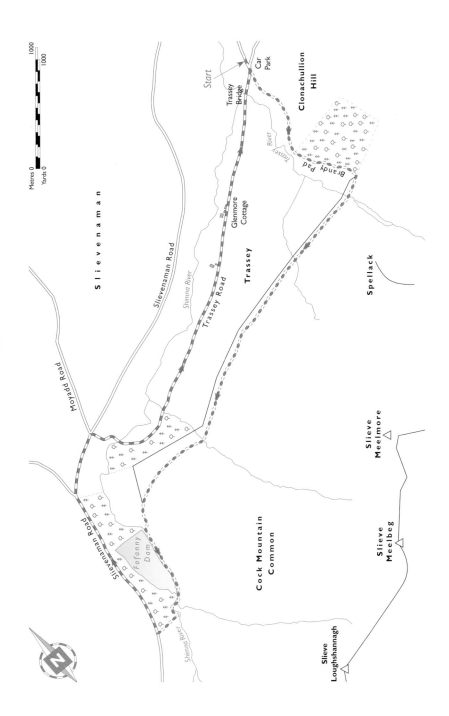

Start

Trassey
Bridge

Car
Park

Clonachullion
Hill

Trassey River

Brandy Pad

Glenmore
Cottage

Trassey

Spellack

Slievenaman

Slievenaman Road

Shimna River

Trassey Road

Moyadd Road

Slievenaman Road

Fofanny
Dam

Cock Mountain
Common

Shimna River

Slieve
Meelmore

Slieve
Meelbeg

Slieve
Loughshannagh

Metres 0
Yards 0

1000

1000

THE TRASSEY TRACK

The Trassey Track Walk consists of a public right of way, that forms part of the Ulster Way, and quiet country roads running along the lower slopes of the Mourne Mountains. Down District Council provides a car park and picnic area close to the entrance. Please refrain from parking on the roadway or from blocking lane and farm entrances.

In the past, smuggled goods were transported along the Trassey Track. These originated at the coast on the eastern side of the mountains. Ponies transported the contraband over the mountains and along the Brandy Pad to the Hare's Gap. From here they went down to the Trassey Track and on to places like Hilltown for further distribution.

The walk starts from the small car park and picnic area at the base of Clonachullion Hill. The Ulster Way joins the road from a lane, coming from Tollymore Forest, just above the car park. Turn left as you walk on to the road. Continue uphill until you reach a gate and large stone stile with an information board that marks the start of the Trassey Track. Climb over the stile and follow the stone path.

A small stream flows beside a section of the track. On the left of the path is a forest. To the right is open land, and there are fine views of the lower slopes of the Mournes. Also, on your right you will

INFORMATION

Distance: 10 km (6 miles).

Start and finish: Car park and picnic area, Clonachullion Hill, off the Bryansford to Kilkeel road.

Terrain: Roads, paths and tracks.

Toilets: Public toilets in Newcastle or Castlewellan.

Refreshments: Shops in the village of Bryansford. Pubs, shops and restaurants in the nearby towns of Newcastle and Castlewellan.

Public transport: Bus service from Newcastle, Castlewellan and Downpatrick. Get off at Tory Bush Picnic Site. This is close to the junction of the Trassey Road and the Kilkeel/Bryansford Road.

The start of the Trassey Track.

notice the Trassey River. This feeds the Shimna River, situated just below the entrance, from the mountains above.

Climb over the next stile and continue uphill along the forest edge towards the wall. At the end of the forest you will come across a gate, stile and wall. After negotiating the stile, turn right and walk along beside the wall. This will take you across the base of the mountain towards Fofanny Dam Reservoir. This stretch of the walk takes you along the foot of the domed Slieve Meelmore. Derived from the Irish, Slieve Meelmore translates as 'the big bare mountain'. A Belfast Water Commissioners' tower tops it, built in 1921 as part of the Mourne Wall.

The Mourne Wall connects the main peaks of the Mournes and marks the boundary of the Belfast Water Commissioners' water catchment area. Water within this area feeds the main reservoirs in the Mournes which in turn feeds Belfast.

Walk along beside the wall across, in places, rough open ground. Several streams cross your path. No single position for crossing those streams exists as it depends on ground and weather conditions at the time. Follow existing tracks and try not to form new ones as this spreads the problem of erosion. I always find the sheep know best. Take time to view the landscape to the north while making your way along the wall. This takes in the beautiful green countryside and in the distance the majestic Slieve Croob.

Heading down from the wall towards Fofanny Dam.

As you near the end of the wall, a stream cuts across your path. Leave the wall just before this point, follow the path towards the stream and cross over. Take the path uphill and follow the waymarked route around the crest of the hill. This is the base of Slieve Meelmore. A small wooded area appears on the other side of the wall below. Soon Fofanny Dam will come into view. This is a beautiful reservoir with another small wood on the opposite side.

Fofanny Dam.

As you approach the dam, cross a stile and walk along an artificially constructed bank that separates the reservoir from a canal.

Walk up this bank and along the side of the reservoir to the opposite end. Then turn right across the stream and walk towards the wood. Enter the wood and keep left along the edge of the trees. At the boundary, turn right, uphill until you see a large ladder stile that will take you into a field. Climb over and walk up the field towards another ladder stile that will take you over a fence and onto the Slievenaman Road.

Turn right on the road, heading north and downhill. As you walk along the road it is delightful to look down through the trees at the reservoir below. Keep on the Slievenaman Road and ignore a fork to your left. A short distance later, as the road veers to the right, you will arrive at a crossroad. Turn right on to the Trassey Road, which is quiet and carries little traffic. Soon you will cross the Shimna River, which flows from here through Tollymore Forest to reach the Irish Sea at Newcastle.

As you walk along, with the river on your left, it is interesting to look up the mountain side and view the route you have just followed. Eventually you will arrive back at the gate where you first joined the Trassey Track. Continue downhill to the car park where your journey started.

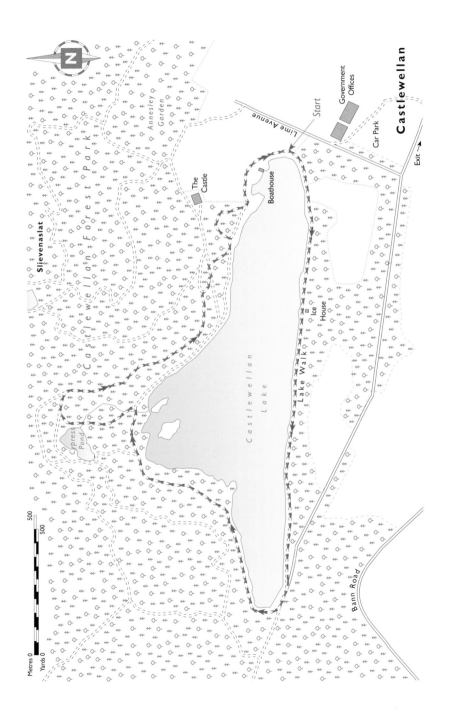

CASTLEWELLAN FOREST PARK

Castlewellan Forest Park is a Department of Agriculture property situated on the outskirts of Castlewellan. The property was previously owned by the Annesley family and was their main place of residence. The park covers an area of 460 hectares of natural beauty enhanced by diverse woodland and a variety of attractive man-made features. The main features of the park are the lake, a castle, the Annesley Garden, National Arboretum and the Grange Yard.

Four waymarked trails of varying length wind through the forest, leading you into some of the park's most beautiful wooded areas. The Lake and Sculpture Trail is described here. This leads you around the lake, is generally level, and is suitable for all ages. Along the route are sculptures created from local materials. The walk begins at the information panel adjacent to the car park beside the lake and is waymarked.

Start by walking west, along the southern side of the lake. After a short distance you will find the first sculpture on your left. It is called 'Dreams and Stones' by Michael Bulfin. The sculpture is arranged in such a way as to create a space, a place to sit and think, to dream. These stones may be 300 million years old and remind you of an ancient burial site.

A little further along the path on the same side you will see sculpture no 2. This is called 'Tobar na Sli' by Cliodna Cussen; the name means 'Well of the Way'. It is made of granite, and praises the pure water from the Mournes. Return to the path and a short distance later, high up on the bank, you will notice sculpture no 3, 'Idirghniomh' by Ned Jackson Smyth. The title means 'Interaction' and represents the interaction

INFORMATION

Distance: 4.8 km (3 miles).

Start and finish: Lakeside car park, Castlewellan Forest Park, signposted from the town of Castlewellan.

Terrain: Forest tracks and paths. Strong shoes or boots recommended.

Toilets: Several within the park.

Refreshments: Restaurant within the stable yard complex (Mar-Oct). Wider choice in Castlewellan.

Public transport: Bus service from Downpatrick and Newcastle.

Opening hours: The park is open all year, 10,00-dusk. Admission charge. Further information, tel 013967 78664.

Castlewellan Castle.

Sculpture No I, 'Dreams and Stones'.

between the carved wooden forms, their environment and the viewer.

As you near the end of the lake you will observe, again on your left, sculpture no 4. This is called 'Dinosaur', by Christos Alaverus, and is a beautiful, realistically shaped wooden monster.

At the end of the road turn right, as directed by the waymarker at the base of a stone wall, and continue across the end of the lake. The path veers right and follows the lake shore. Trees line both sides of this section of the walk. It then leaves the side of the lake and climbs uphill.

Sculpture No 6 'Sacred Grove'.

You then enter a typically dark coniferous section of the wood. Walk downhill to the side of the lake. Just offshore is a small tree-clad island. Between the path and the lake you will find sculpture no 5, 'Temple and Nest' by Verhulst and Gerrie Goossens. This is based on primitive architecture, a temple-house on land and a nest in the water.

Just past this point, on a bank above the path, is sculpture no 6, 'Sacred Grove' by Graeme Hall, positioned by the artist so that it blends into the natural environment. The artist sees it as a shape that draws you towards it, suggesting the entrance to a tomb, or passageway, which may or may not exist. You will have to find out.

After your investigation, return to the lakeside path and turn left. A short distance later, a waymark directs you uphill to your left away from the lake. As you near the top you will find sculpture no 7 in a clearing on your right. It is called 'Homage to the Larch' by Betty Maguire, and is described by the artist as a place which people can enter and relate to the many wonders of the forest.

On the opposite side is a pond called Cypress Pond. The whole area is like a small pleasure ground. Continue uphill and to the right, keeping to the main path, until it joins another track, then turn right as directed. Walk along the ridge high above the lake. Just below this ridge, on your right, is the 8th sculpture, my favourite, 'Arboreal Throne' by Aaron Fowler. This is in the shape of a throne high on a bank above the lake. Sit here, as the artist invites, look and listen and feel humble in comparison.

When you are ready, return to the path and continue until you are directed downhill towards the lake. This is a less formal path that travels down through the trees until it joins a vehicle track. Turn left at this point. A short distance later, a waymark directs you further downhill to the lakeside path. Keep to the main path, then at a fork take a grass path to the left. Just opposite the next directional sign is sculpture no 9, 'Piece for a Maple Tree' by Kathy Herbert – difficult to locate as it is sited on the ground below a maple tree.

Rejoin the path and a short distance later go left as directed. Look out for a canine feature. Turn right just past this point into an open lawn area. Facing you is the final sculpture, no 10 'Stone head with four faces' by Anastasios Giokas. The granite head symbolises the links between youth and age, in the international bond of friendship, stretching to the four corners of the earth.

At the opposite end of the lawn go through an opening, this marks the end of the sculpture trail. The castle is high above on your left. Take an informal path back towards the lake, then go left along the water's edge towards the car park where the walk began.

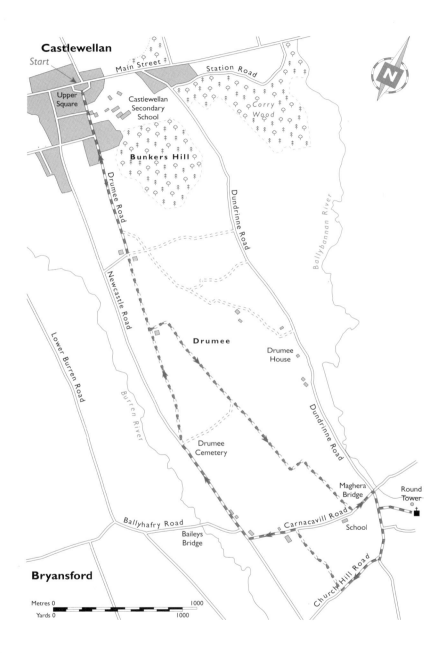

DRUMEE COUNTRYSIDE WALK

Drumee Countryside Walk is on the outskirts of the town of Castlewellan, which lies in the foothills of the Mourne Mountains. Castlewellan is a market town that serves this beautiful farming area of County Down. Drumee is the name of the main townland through which the walk passes.

The Drumee Walk is part of an old and intricate transport network connecting the settlements of Castlewellan, Annesborough, Maghera, Dundrum, Bryansford and Newcastle. These lanes served the town on market days and on Sundays were used by people going to their place of worship. They also offered the shortest, easiest routes for a horse and cart, or the traveller on foot. Today these old rural routes offer peaceful country walks away from the busy main roads.

The walk starts from the car park in the Upper Square. From here you take the Circular Road which is in the south-eastern corner of the square. This road leads away from the town towards the coast. As you leave the town, the road becomes the Drumee Road. Walk past the first Public Footpath sign and continue downhill until you arrive at a riding stable. The road veers to the right at this point; ignore this and follow the route signposted straight ahead.

INFORMATION

Distance: 9.3 km (5.8 miles).

Start and finish: Car park, Upper Square, Castlewellan (on the A25 between Downpatrick and Newry).

Terrain: Road, tracks and paths. Strong shoes or boots recommended as parts of the walk can be muddy and uneven.

Toilets: Upper Square, Castlewellan.

Refreshments: Wide choice in Castlewellan.

Public transport: Bus services from Downpatrick, Newry and Newcastle.

Path from the Carnacavill Road.

Continue until a public footpath sign shows another path to the left; take this route. The route is typical of the stonewalled lanes of the Mourne uplands. Follow the path, which after a short distance turns sharply to the right. Take time to look at the countryside around you. View the Irish Sea in the distance straight ahead, the Mourne Mountains to your right and the colourful patchwork of farmland between.

This is a straight stretch of path which descends slowly towards the coast and the seaside resort of Newcastle. Eventually you will reach a junction with another lane which veers right, towards a large farmhouse. Ignore this route and take the waymarked path to the left. This is another long, straight stretch of lane which eventually turns sharp left and then right before reaching the Carnacavill Road.

Maghera Churches.

At the junction with this road, turn left and walk towards a crossroads. Here you will see a signpost saying 'Maghera Old Church and Round Tower'. Follow this sign which will take you on to the Dundrine Road. A short distance later you will see another sign directing you up a driveway to the church and a round tower.

Maghera is a typical rural Church of Ireland parish church and although quite old is still in use today. It has a very interesting graveyard and the ruin of an earlier church immediately to the rear of the present one is worth investigating. Look around the headstones and you will soon become conversant with the names of the families of the district. Also, take time to look at the remains of the old round tower. It is inside the field to the left as you approach the church. This would be the oldest section of this ancient religious settlement.

After visiting the church return to the Dundrine Road, turn left, walk a few hundred metres, then take a right turn onto Church Hill Road. This is a narrow, quiet road. After walking a few hundred metres, turn right as directed by a public path signpost. Walk up this lane, known as Smiley's Loanan. It will take you past a house and then on to a narrow tree- and hedge-lined track. The remainder of this lane is quite narrow and can be a squeeze if you meet horses coming the other way. Don't worry, from experience you can pass.

Follow this path until it returns you to the Carnacavill Road. At the road turn left; this will take you to the main Castlewellan to Newcastle Road. Turn right when you arrive at the main road and walk back towards Castlewellan. The traffic can be quite fast on this busy road. However the road is broad, and has a wide grass verge set back from the side of the road. Stay on the verge as it provides a safe footpath to walk on.

Continue as far as Drumee Cemetery, which is a graveyard set back from the road behind a high stone wall. Look for a public footpath signpost with one sign pointing right and the other straight ahead towards the town. Take the grassy path towards Castlewellan. This is a narrow path that climbs uphill and at a slight angle to the main road. From here you again get a beautiful panoramic view of the mountains, the surrounding countryside and the town of Castlewellan straight ahead.

Early section of route.

As you approach a house at the top of the hill you will recognise the lane in front of you as the one you first walked down. Follow the waymark post back towards Castlewellan and retrace your steps to the Drumee Road. Continue past the Riding Stables and up the hill back to the Upper Square and the car park where the walk started.

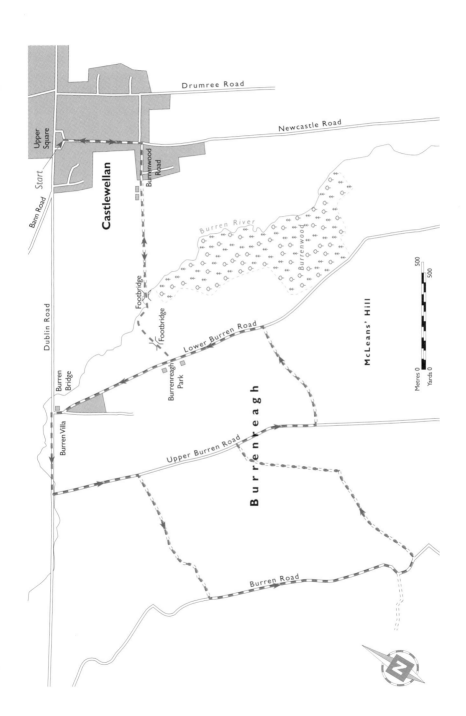

BURRENREAGH COUNTRYSIDE WALK

Burrenreagh Countryside Walk is on the outskirts of the town of Castlewellan. This walk extends to the south-west and more directly on the foothills to the Mourne Mountains. Burrenreagh is the name of the main townland in the area covered by the walks.

This network, like the Drumee network, served the market town of Castlewellan with a transport system of lanes and paths. Local people have likened Castlewellan to the centre of a wheel and the lanes as the spokes moving out from the centre. The town still holds a market day once a month and an annual Horse Fair every May, bringing prosperity to traders and local shops.

Castlewellan now also hosts the annual Down District Walking Festival (normally held at the beginning of August). This is a very successful weekend attracting walkers from all over the world. These lane networks form a very important part of that festival, as they allow participants some contrast with the more energetic walks on the nearby Mournes.

The walk starts this time in the Lower Square, to the Newry side of the town. From outside the Chestnut Bar, take the Newcastle Road out of the town. A few hundred metres from the square, turn right into Burrenwood Road. This leads past some new houses to

INFORMATION

Distance: 8.4 km (5.25 miles).

Start and finish: Lower Square car park, Castlewellan.

Terrain: Road, tracks and paths. Strong shoes or boots recommended as parts of the walk can be muddy and uneven.

Toilets: Upper Square, Castlewellan.

Refreshments: Wide choice in Castlewellan.

Public transport: Bus services from Downpatrick, Newry and Newcastle.

Ruin of old home.

Cow Lane. From here you will see a public footpath signpost directing you down the lane. Cow Lane is a grass-topped lane with stone walls on each side. It takes you downhill and into the open countryside.

Near the bottom of the hill you will find a stile that takes you into the field. Go over the stile, turn right and walk towards the bottom of the field. Look for a small wooden footbridge and cross over into the next field. Follow the field boundary to the right until you reach a waymarker showing that the path crosses the field at right angles to your present direction. Take this route and walk across the field where you will find another wooden footbridge that takes you over a small stream in the middle of the field. Continue uphill in the same direction until you reach the field boundary. Then step over another stile on to the Lower Burren Road.

A typical path with drystone walls to either side.

Turn right at this point and walk towards the Dublin Road. When you reach the Dublin Road turn left. This can be a busy and fast road, so keep an eye on the traffic. Luckily you are only on this road for a few hundred metres before you turn left again into the Upper Burren Road. Walk uphill from this point to the top of the hill, where you will see a signpost indicating that a public footpath is on your right.

Take this path, called Caskell Lane, and follow it over the top of the hill. Stop anywhere on this lane and look around you at the beautiful scenery. You have a wonderful panoramic view that takes in all of the surrounding countryside. From here you can really feel at one with nature and drift back in time to when time itself stood still.

A distant view of the Mournes.

Continue to the end of the lane until you reach Burren Road, then turn left and walk until another signpost shows a public footpath on your left. Again take this path, called Rock Lane, and follow it over the top of the hill then down towards some houses. The views here are similar to the previous lane, only you are walking in the opposite direction. Weave your way past the houses by following the track. Keep going straight ahead and do not turn off the lane. A few hundred metres past the last house, the lane veers sharply to the right and down a steep hill back to the Upper Burren Road.

Turn right at this junction and walk along the road until a public footpath sign indicates a path on your left. Take this path, which leads you downhill past a house onto a narrow lane. Follow the lane to the Lower Burren Road, then turn left and walk back to a public footpath sign. The sign will direct you over a stile on your right and into the field that first brought you from Cow Lane to the Lower Burren Road.

Climb over the stile and retrace your steps to the wooden footbridge. Continue to the field boundary, where a waymark post sends you to the right. Walk around the field boundary and back to the wooden footbridge that you crossed at the beginning. Cross the bridge into the next field, then along the stone ditch, on your left, to the stile that returns you to Cow Lane.

Walk uphill to the top of the lane, into Burrenwood Road. The lane is quite steep and tiring, especially at the finish of the walk. Continue to the end of the road and onto the Newcastle Road, then turn left towards the Lower Square and the point where the walk started.

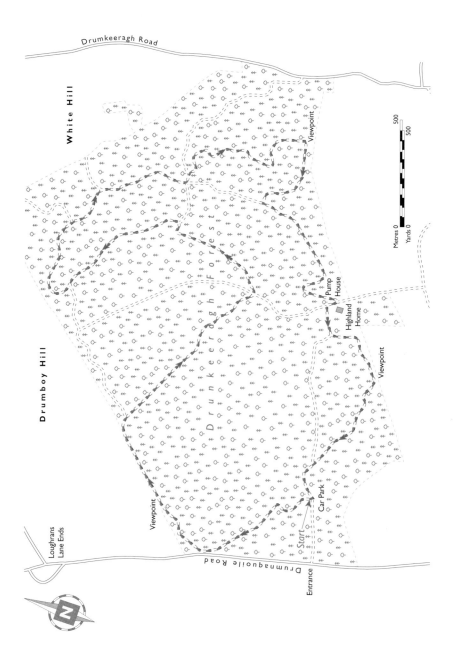

DRUMKEERAGH FOREST PARK

Drumkeeragh Forest Park is a Department of Agriculture property, situated on the eastern slopes of Slieve Croob, near the town of Ballynahinch. It is one of six forest parks in County Down managed by the Department. Slieve Croob lies to the north of the Mourne Mountains, surrounded by the drumlin country that is a feature of Down.

The forest covers an area of 200 hectares with an elevation that rises from 190 m to 310 m. The predominant species is Sitka spruce with Norway spruce, European larch, western red cedar, Douglas and noble fir, Scots, Corsican and lodgepole pines also present. Land in this area is not suitable for growing broadleaved trees because of its high elevation and poor soils.

Drumkeeragh is now entering its second rotation and a programme of felling and replanting is underway. Conifer forests are a major habitat of the woodcock and the 'new' forest, that will receive greater emphasis on wildlife conservation, should produce a greater diversity of bird species.

INFORMATION

Distance: 6.7 km (4 miles).

Start and finish: Car park off the Drumnaquoile Road near Ballynahinch.

Terrain: Forest paths and tracks. Strong shoes or boots recommended.

Toilets: No toilets are available within the Park.

Refreshments: No facilities within the Park. Pubs and restaurants in nearby Seeconnell Centre or the towns of Dromara, Clough and Ballynahinch.

Public transport: Nil.

Car park area within the Forest Park, with Slieve Croob in the background.

A feature of the park is the number of excellent viewing points spaced around the perimeter and the experience of walking through an active working forest. The main entrance is off the Drumnaquoile Road just below Slieve Croob. Facilities are limited to small informal car parks and a few picnic tables.

Walkers use the park for recreation and horse owners, permits only, come to exercise their horses.

Within the park are three circular waymarked paths of varying lengths. A map at the main car park shows the layout of the paths and how they relate to each other. This walk combines two of these waymarked walks because they cover the best viewing points and show excellent examples of the different trees and forestry management.

Car park with Slieve Croob in the background.

The walk starts at the main car park beside a notice board showing the various walks through the forest. Taking the red route, head towards the westerly boundary of the park. The path takes you past the concrete bases of an old caravan park attached to the park. It then swings right, and uphill, to one of the main forest tracks. Turn left at the track and after a few hundred metres you will reach a gate beside the main road. Veer right, and walk uphill away from the road and into the woodland.

At this point the path is quite steep. When you reach the top of the path it begins to level out and run along a stone wall boundary. Here you will find the first of many viewing points that look from the park out towards the open countryside. Because the forest is situated on high ground, the views are impressive and extend far into the distance to Belfast and beyond.

After a short distance the path turns east and again uphill. This is a dark stretch of the path where the trees are mature and meet overhead. The park unfortunately has a dark side to its recent history and an unofficial memorial to a femme-fatale event is eerily situated at the side of the path.

Follow the path uphill over the top and downhill again until you reach another path. Walk straight across the intersection, veer left and downhill. At the time of writing this point marked the edge of the area being cleared for replanting. The path then veers sharply right and down a short steep hill towards the junction with yet another path. When you reach the junction, turn left along the crest of the hill. This will take you back again towards the western boundary.

As it nears the boundary the path climbs, then veers right and downhill in an easterly direction. Keep walking straight ahead and ignore two smaller paths on your right. Turn left at the next crossroads, before climbing again, this time into a mature wooded area. A narrow path takes you through this section of the forest and around the summit of a hill that dominates the eastern side of the park. From the summit the path will take you back towards the centre of the park where the trees have been cleared.

When you reach the next junction turn left, as directed by the waymark, onto one of the main forest roads. Continue along this road uphill, past the Pump House and the Highland Home. At the next red waymark post, turn left instead of right as directed. This detour

A section of the forest road.

will take you to the boundary wall and more selected viewpoints. The forestry service provide seats at all the major viewpoints and these are well worth using. From this side of the park you can look over Guinness Mountain and Edendarriff Mountain. In the distance you can see right across the district and pick out the towns and villages. Downpatrick is very prominent.

Continue along the path, away from the boundary and downhill to join a larger forest track. From here, turn right and follow the waymarked path back to the car park where the walk started.

Metres 0 ————————— 250
Yards 0 ————————— 250

N

Entrance

R o w a l l a n e

(N a t i o n a l   T r u s t)

Car Park

Start

Pond

Rowallane

The Paddock

Holly Rock

Walled Garden

The Haggard

Spring Ground

The Hospital

Old Wood

Pleasure Grounds

Bandstand

Tro Hill

New Ground

The Rock Garden

The Bishop's Rock

ROWALLANE GARDEN

Rowallane Garden, 'a garden for all seasons', is a National Trust property. It is situated 17.5 km south of Belfast, on the southern outskirts of the town of Saintfield, amid the rolling drumlins of County Down. Formerly a farm belonging to the Reverend John Moore, who acquired it in the 1860s, it is now one of the foremost gardens in the British Isles.

John Moore gradually enlarged his farmhouse, added the stable block, and planted the pleasure grounds. On his death in 1903 he left Rowallane to his nephew, Hugh Armytage Moore, who had a rare gift for planning and a great eye for plants. The garden has a profusion of azaleas and rhododendrons, naturalised bulbs, rare trees, specimen conifers.

Rowallane was originally a private garden and the Trust has sought to retain this atmosphere for today's visitor. Ask for a brochure and map at the ticket kiosk when you arrive.

Start the walk by leaving the car park from the pedestrian exit nearest the main drive. Beside the exit is an information panel. Cross a small stone bridge on to the main entrance drive. Then turn right up the gentle hill towards the house.

Walk past the front of the house, then take a small gravel path to the right. In the middle is a sun dial and after checking the time (don't forget to add summer time), turn left into the walled garden. Take time to walk around and explore all the paths and sheltered corners of this very picturesque garden, then leave through an arch at the opposite end. This leads into the outer walled garden. Turn left at this point and walk towards the old potting sheds, now used as an interpretation display area.

INFORMATION

Distance: 3.2 km (2 miles).

Start and finish: Main car park, Rowallane, signposted off the A7 road 1.5 km south of Saintfield.

Terrain: Road and paths. No special footwear needed, though grass areas can be slippery.

Toilets: Outside the stable yard.

Refreshments: Restaurant to the rear of the stable buildings (Easter and summer only, hours vary). Wider choice in Saintfield.

Public transport: Bus services from Downpatrick and Belfast.

Opening hours: Apr-Oct, Mon-Fri 1030-1800, Sat-Sun 1400-1800. Nov-Mar Mon-Fri 1030-1700. Admission charge (National Trust members free).

View of The Haggard.

Turn right past the sheds into an area known as The Haggard, the stackyard of the original Rowallane farm. Follow the main estate path around to the left of the grass area and through a gateway framed with two large stone pillars.

Colourful scene in the walled garden.

Take the grass path to the right, away from the estate path, and walk down the centre of the grass area, known as the Spring Ground. As you pass two small outcrops of rock, one on each side, turn right between some trees and visit Trio Hill. Keep left and walk uphill to the top of this area, then left through a gap in a stone wall. Walk down this path, taking time to investigate a large stone formation on your left, called The Bishop's Rock.

Continue straight ahead to the Rock Garden. Circumnavigate this area using the system of paths provided. Return to the path on which you approached the Rock Garden, cross over and walk through a gateway back towards the Spring Ground. Keep to a grass path that branches to the right and passes through a small pedestrian gate that forms an opening in a low stone wall. This gate marks the entrance to the Old Wood.

Keep straight ahead until you reach the corner of another stone wall. These walls are part of the old field pattern of the original farm. Walk past the corner and turn right through a pedestrian gate, this area contains the Handkerchief Tree, one of the most famous species of tree in the garden. In late May, remarkable flowers with protruding red stamens in a rounded head appear, each being subtended by two large creamy bracts giving the unique 'handkerchief' effect.

Follow the mown path, keeping to the right until it joins another path. Turn left at this point and walk through an opening in another stone wall into an area known as the Holly Rock.

Go straight across this area and through another wall opening into The Paddock. This area is kept as a meadow and has several mown paths. Follow one of these paths to the opposite left-hand corner. Pass through a gate in the stone wall. Walk straight ahead until you reach the main entrance drive, then turn left and back to the main administrative building.

Return to the sundial, and instead of turning left into the walled garden, go straight ahead along the side of the building. This leads to a large open semi-wooded grass area called the Pleasure Grounds. Continue walking until you reach an estate track. Turn left and follow the track, ignoring the branch to the left. Continue walking up the side of a wooded area and past an old Victorian bandstand.

A short distance later the track veers to the left and fades out. At this point branch to the right and up a bank, then follow a grass path that swings to the right. Keep left at the next path junction. This new path continues to swing to the right and eventually comes out of the trees into the central grass area just opposite the bandstand.

Wildlife in the pleaseure grounds.

No formal path exists at this point. Walk down the left-hand side of the central grass avenue until you reach an embankment. Turn right at the top of the slope and walk for a short distance before taking a small path, to the left, downhill between the trees. Follow this path to the right and round a small pond.

This water feature is a pleasant surprise hidden behind the trees. In the centre are two small tree-covered islands. Walk around the pond over a wooden bridge then continue back to the open fairway. Keep left and continue along the side of the trees until you reach a vehicle track. Turn left and follow the track to the car park where the walk began.

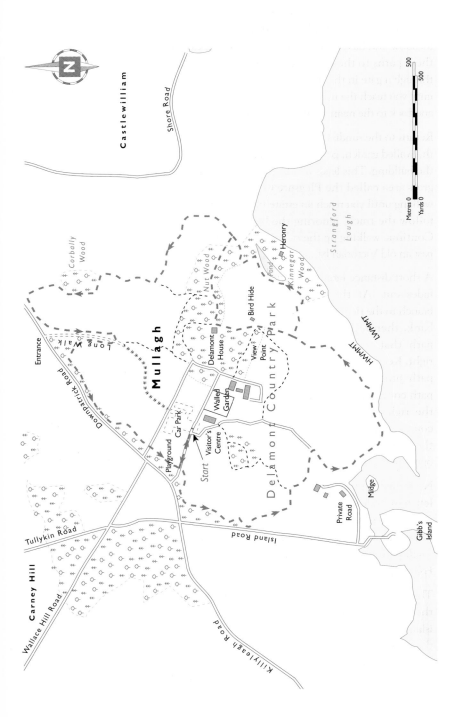

DELAMONT COUNTRY PARK

Delamont Country Park is situated on the shores of Strangford Lough and is within the Strangford Lough Area of Outstanding Natural Beauty. The lough, which has recently been designated a Marine Nature Reserve, is also world famous for its natural beauty and sailing activities. Most of the park is owned and managed by the Countryside Development Section of Down District Council.

Delamont is one of the fastest growing visitor attractions in Ireland. Visitors come to enjoy the beautiful views across Strangford Lough, to walk in the peace and tranquillity, and to spend quality time with their family. A naturally landscaped playground has made the park very popular with children. Beside the playground is a large car park surrounded by picnic tables and an open grass area for informal play.

Looking from the car park, you will notice a modern building called the Visitor Centre. This building includes the warden's office, a gift shop, information point and toilets. Across from this building is the education centre and exhibition room. Beside all of this is a curious glass dome or 'Siglu', also privately managed and used to provide refreshment.

Behind the Visitor Centre are a walled garden and some old farm buildings. Within the Walled Garden is a privately managed display garden. The garden has a variety of trees and shrubs, laid out in various formal settings, most of which visitors can buy at the Garden Shop. In addition the garden has a small playground, maze, glasshouses and tea rooms.

Delamont has many waymarked walks, all suitable for a pushchair, ranging from 1 km to 9.6 km in length. Many of the routes pass through unspoilt mature woodland, along the foreshore and open parkland where the public can walk through the sheep grazing in the meadows.

INFORMATION

Distance: 5.2 km (3.25 miles).

Start and finish: Car park, Delamont, off the Downpatrick Road.

Terrain: Road, tracks and paths. Strong shoes or boots recommended.

Toilets: At the Visitor Centre.

Refreshments: Tea rooms in the walled garden, only open during certain hours. The 'Siglu' by arrangement. Pubs, shops and restaurants in the nearby towns of Killyleagh and Downpatrick.

Public transport: Bus service from Downpatrick and Comber.

Opening hours: Dawn until dusk.

Admission charge: There is a charge for cars, buses and motorcycles.

View across the Quoile Estuary with Slieve Patrick in the background.

I have chosen the Long Walk as I feel it lets the visitor get a complete picture of the park at its best. Begin the walk at the main car park and follow the light blue waymark sign towards the western boundary and the Killyleagh to Downpatrick Road. This path leads to the rear of a small former estate house. Turn left at the end of the path and go through a gateway. Always be sure to close all gates behind you on this walk, as this stops the sheep from straying. Walk around the rear of the property and then uphill and through another gate into the first open meadow.

The view across the Quoile Estuary from the park.

Follow the path as it winds across the bottom of the meadow and through another gateway. A small stream flows beside the path and under the Island Road that runs down the side of the park to Mullagh Quay.

Continue walking across the next field and uphill towards the next field boundary, then keep right through another gate. From this spot you can get a very pleasant view of Mullagh Quay, the Quoile Nature Reserve and the Mournes beyond. Follow the path downhill across two fields and through a large timber gate on to the main path leading down to the foreshore. Turn right and walk along this route, veering left at the bottom, and continue until stopped by another large wooden gate.

After passing through the gate you enter a large grass meadow that stretches right up to the top of the hill. Climb the hill. From here the views over the Quoile estuary, Strangford Lough and the countryside beyond are truly magnificent. Two-thirds of the way up you will see a fingerpost directing you downhill towards the shore and a wooded area.

This is Kinnegar Wood, and it contains one of the largest heronries in Ireland. The path is seasonal and is closed when the herons are breeding from March to July. During this period, visitors are asked to follow the path up to the top of the hill. This has its consolations as this section of the path network is equally as pleasant. You also get a chance to observe the heronry and its associated pond from the purpose-built hide. At the top of the hill there is also a lookout tower and a Rath. All are worth a visit.

Following the directional arm of the fingerpost, take the path down to the wood through a new plantation. You will pass through several kissing gates to the bottom of a large field which again stretches to the top of the hill. Follow the path along the bottom of the field and past a beautiful large pond that extends along the length of the heronry. Over the pond are several boardwalks that allow you to observe the flora and fauna.

The pond below the heronry.

Leave this area by following the path out of the field and into Nut Wood. Continue around the wood and over the next field. Then keep with the path which runs along the park boundary and uphill to a small wooded area called Corbally Wood. Walk around the wood to the opposite side then through another new plantation and downhill towards the park entrance. The path then follows the main entrance drive to the first corner, where you turn right and asross the main entrance road and into a long avenue of trees called the Long Walk. This was the former servants or tradesman's entrance to Delamont House.

After you walk along the path and through the trees you will be heading back towards the Downpatrick Road. The path then runs along the side of the road through some more trees that border the large meadow. Follow the path over a small stream at the boundary wall and then through a small wooded area to the old entrance road. Cross the road, through another wooded area and past the children's playground. Turn left at the lane you first walked down and back to the car park where the walk began.

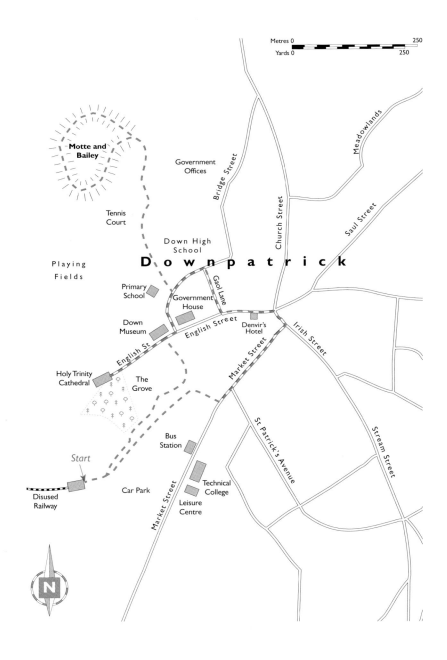

Metres 0   250
Yards 0   250

Motte and Bailey

Government Offices

Bridge Street

Meadowlands

Church Street

Saul Street

Tennis Court

Down High School

D o w n p a t r i c k

Playing Fields

Primary School

Gaol Lane

Government House

Down Museum

English Street

Denvir's Hotel

Irish Street

English St

Holy Trinity Cathedral

The Grove

Market Street

Bus Station

St Patrick's Avenue

Stream Street

Start

Car Park

Market Street

Technical College

Leisure Centre

Disused Railway

N

DOWNPATRICK
HISTORICAL TRAIL

This walk explores one of Ireland's oldest towns. Downpatrick was the County Town of Down and is built on several hills beside the River Quoile that flows into Strangford Lough. Its name comes from dun, the Irish word for a fort, and Padraig or Patrick, the patron saint of Ireland.

Start the walk where visitors would have arrived in the town many years ago, at the newly created Downpatrick Steam Railway. This is near the site of the old railway station, which was originally built in the 1870s by the Belfast and County Down Railway. The current project was created to form a realistic museum of the town's railway heritage. Try to arrange your visit to coincide with one of the open days at the station.

When leaving the station, turn left and walk along a timber fence to an open grass and woodland park, planted by Edward Southwell in 1740. This area, known as The Grove, is where John Wesley (1703-91), the founder of Methodism, preached. Follow the lower path until a sign directs you uphill to Down Cathedral and the Down County Museum. The hill is quite steep and you will have to climb some steps at the top before reaching the Mall.

Turn left and walk up the Mall towards the Cathedral. On your left is the Southwell Charity, one of the best examples of early Georgian building in Ulster. There

INFORMATION

Distance: 5km (3 miles).

Start and finish: At the Railway Museum, at the rear of Market Street car park.

Terrain: Road, tracks and paths. Strong shoes recommended as the ground can be muddy at the Mound of Down.

Toilets: In the main car park.

Refreshments: Wide choice in Downpatrick.

Public transport: Bus services to and from all main towns.

Opening hours: These vary, and it is best to enquire locally, or by contacting the Tourist Information Centre on 01396 612233. Other useful numbers: Down County Museum, 01396 615218. Down Railway Museum, 01396 615779/617517. Down Cathedral, 01396 614922.

Down County Museum.

were schools for boys and girls, one at each end of the almshouse. Continue up the Mall and note a carved cross on a grass area in front of the cathedral dating from the tenth or eleventh century.

Evidence of Neolithic and Bronze Age settlements were found on the hill. This was followed by an Iron Age hill fort, making it an important political capital for the area. A church has existed here since very early Christian times and has had obvious connections with St Patrick, who is buried beside the cathedral.

Down Cathedral.

Before the Norman conquest by John de Courcy, there was an Augustinian monastery on the site. They were replaced in 1177 by Benedictines. The cathedral was burned and pillaged on several occasions but was substantially rebuilt as you see it today in 1829. It is worth looking around the cathedral; guided tours and a gift shop are available.

Walk back along the Mall to Down County Museum, housed in the former Down County gaol, which was built between 1789 and 1796. It is the most complete surviving Irish gaol of its type and period. Behind the high perimeter walls are the former gatehouses, residential and service buildings and a cell block. For much of the 19th century it was used by the South Down Militia, and troops were billeted here during both World Wars. The best-known prisoner was the United Irishman, Thomas Russell, was was hanged at the gateway in 1803 and buried in the local parish church.

When leaving the Museum, turn left and left again into Mount Crescent. Around the back of the recently restored 19th century Courthouse until you reach a sign directing you, downhill and to the left, to the Mound of Down. This is the second principal dun or fort in the area and is on the edge of the marshes that flank the River Quoile. Continue downhill to a small car park at the bottom.

Climb over a stone stile and continue straight along the boundary fence to an interpretive panel. This describes the history of the mound and gives directions as to how to explore the structure. It advises three walks; do follow them if you can, as this is the only way you will fully appreciate this enormous earthwork.

After viewing the mound, retrace your steps uphill to the back of the Courthouse. Turn left and continue until you are in front of a formidable gatehouse. This was once the entrance to the County Gaol and now leads to Down High School. The gaol was built in 1831 to replace the one now housing the museum.

Down High School entrance, formerly part of the County Gaol.

Opposite is a narrow passage called Gaol Lane. Walk down this lane, back to English Street. The tall 18th century houses are characteristic of the old part of Downpatrick. Many of these houses were connected to the church and the administration of the region. Names such as Clergy Widows Houses, Customs House and the Deanery verify this.

Denvir's Hotel, towards the foot of the street, merits special mention, and perhaps a visit if you are in need of refreshment. The building dates from the 17th century, and during recent renovations, two medieval fireplaces were uncovered and restored. Denvir's was also the starting point for the first passenger coach service from Downpatrick to Belfast, in 1809.

Continue downhill to the busy intersection. This has long been the hub of Downpatrick and is where the old settlements of English Street, Scotch Street and Irish Street met. Keep right and follow the footpath round and into Market Street. Built in 1846, this is now the main shopping thoroughfare and road through the town. Before that date, the area was covered in water during high tides, and small vessels could discharge their cargoes here.

Walk down Market Street back to the car park where the walk started.

INDEX

Published by The Stationery Office Limited and available from:

The Stationery Office Bookshops
16 Arthur Street, Belfast BT1 4GD
01232 238451 Fax 01232 235401
71 Lothian Road, Edinburgh EH3 9AZ
0131 228 4181 Fax 0131 622 7017
123 Kingsway, London WC2B 6PQ
0171 430 1671 Fax 0171 831 1326
68-69 Bull Street, Birmingham B4 6AD
0121 236 9696 Fax 0121 236 9699
33 Wine Street, Bristol BS1 2BQ
0117 926 4306 Fax 0117 929 4515
9-21 Princess Street, Manchester M60 8AS
0161 834 7201 Fax 0161 833 0634
The Stationery Office Oriel Bookshop
The Friary, Cardiff CF1 4AA
01222 395548 Fax 01222 384347

The Stationery Office publications are also available from:

The Publications Centre
(mail, telephone and fax orders only)
PO Box 276, London SW8 5DT
General enquiries 0171 873 0011

Accredited Agents
(see Yellow Pages)

and through good booksellers

Printed in Scotland for The Stationery Office by CC No. 70343 C25, 11/98